THE
FINAL
ACT

G. Steve Kinnard

THE FINAL ACT

A BIBLICAL LOOK AT END-TIME PROPHECY

DPI

DISCIPLESHIP
PUBLICATIONS
INTERNATIONAL

The Final Act
© 2000 by Discipleship Publications International
One Merrill Street, Woburn, Mass. 01801

Material for this edition, which has been significantly revised and expanded, was previously published under the title *666, Armageddon, the Antichrist and Other Apocalyptic Mysteries* © 1999 by the New York City Church of Christ. Permission to expand and reprint was kindly granted to DPI.

Printed in the United States of America

ISBN: 1-57782-140-8

Book Design: Chad Crossland

In life, you bump into only a handful of special people who touch you in such a way that your life takes a different direction after you meet them. You find only a few special friends that become friends for life. These people become your heroes. They seem bigger than life.

I dedicate this book to two such people:
Mike and Anne-Brigitte Taliaferro.

Mike and Anne-Brigitte, your love drew Leigh and me to the movement of God. You have been a constant source of inspiration, encouragement and friendship. You have always been an upward call to us. Words cannot express all that we owe you. So, let me simply say, "Thanks!"

Contents

Acknowledgments

A word of thanks
to Steve Tetrault and Janice Smith,
for their work on the first edition;

to John Hanes,
for his helpful suggestions;

to Robert and Patricia Shaheen,
for their support, friendship and encouragement;

to Steve and Lisa Johnson
and the New York ministry staff,
for allowing me to research, write and teach;

to Kelly Petre, Kim Hanson, Chad Crossland
and the staff at DPI,
for taking this book and making it better;

and to Leigh, Chelsea and Daniel,
for allowing me to sit in my cave and write—
you always make me smile.

Apocalyptic Booger-Bears

Doomsday prophets
Prognosticate
They pontificate
Prepare yourself
The end is near
As Chicken Little
He runs for cover
To cover himself
Ask not for whom
The death bell tolls
It tolls for me
It tolls for thee
The dragon beast
Prepares a feast
With steeled knife
He waits for thee.

Soothsayers slay
They slay tomorrow
As tock-tick-tock
How time does fly
The Final curtain
Prepares to drop
Drop on the clock
Of millennium time
Like counting backward
To 2,000
Computers crash
The sun turns black
The earth quakes
The earth shakes
The moon turns red
Up rise the dead

I'm scared
Scared stiff
I'm scared
Scared stiff
Of 666
Armageddon
The Mark of the Beast
And other
Big, bad
Apocalyptic
Booger-Bears

I'm scared
Scared stiff
I'm scared
Scared stiff
Of 666
Armageddon
The Mark of the Beast
And other
Big, bad
Apocalyptic
Booger-Bears

Nostradamus
Writes in symbols
While Edgar Cayce
Slumbers on
Fortune cookies
New World Order
Illuminati
Let's bang the gong
Nyack's White Witch
Reading tea leaves
With Ouiji boards
And tarot cards
Double the fortune
On Palm Sunday
A cashless society
Uses credit cards

I'm scared
Scared stiff
I'm scared
Scared stiff
Of 666
Armageddon
The Mark of the Beast
And other
Big, bad
Fat, hairy
Demonic
Diabolical
Apocalyptic
Booger-Bears

–G. *Steve Kinnard*

Introduction

When the trumpet of the Lord shall sound,
And time shall be no more,
And the morning breaks eternal bright and fair,
When the saved of earth shall gather,
Over on the other shore,
And the roll is called up yonder; I'll be there.

"When the Roll Is Called up Yonder"
James Black, 1921

When I was a kid growing up in the mainline Church of Christ in middle Tennessee, I had a Sunday school teacher in the tenth grade who attempted to teach us the book of Revelation. This was around the time that Hal Lindsey released *The Late Great Planet Earth*. There was a buzz in the air about end-time prophecy, the Rapture, Armageddon, 666 and the mark of the beast, the 144,000 and the Antichrist. I thought Revelation was the coolest book of the Bible; after all, it contained blood, dragons, a sword being fired from someone's mouth, plagues and the four horsemen. I went into this Sunday school class with great anticipation and excitement, feeling that all my answers about the book of Revelation would now be answered. I left the class more confused than ever about end-time prophecy.

As a result, I began to explore premillennialism. I watched Garner Ted Armstrong's television show produced by the Worldwide Church of God. Armstrong was a full-blown dispensational premillennialist. He saw apocalyptic signs in news items from around the world. I subscribed to *The Plain Truth*, Armstrong's magazine that foretold apocalyptic events. I began to talk with Jehovah's Witnesses concerning their view of the end-time. I read their magazine *The Watchtower* and bought and read many of their publications. I purchased a *Scofield Reference Bible* because the notes in this Bible delineated premillennial theory. Growing up in an amillennial environment I noticed one sure thing about premillennialists: their view of the end of time was much more exciting and dramatic than my amillennial view. But was it Biblical?

This book will examine beliefs surrounding the end of time. There are many such beliefs, from beliefs that Mother Earth will sprout deadly viruses to avenge the pollution of the environment (the swamp-revenge motif), to beliefs that extraterrestrials are waiting around the corner to invade the planet (*The X-Files,* "I want to believe" scenario), to beliefs that a giant meteor is headed toward the planet (the Hollywood destruction-film genre). At the dawn of a new millennium, of course such beliefs become more prevalent.

Although many of these end-of-the-world scenarios are interesting to examine (and I personally enjoy reading the books and watching the television shows and movies generated by these ideas), this book will concentrate on the Biblical and theological teaching concerning the end of time. Every now and then we will chase a rabbit if it interests us.

Shortly before the end of the year 1999, I was walking with my good friend Steve Johnson through the Barnes and Noble bookstore in Palisades Shopping Center close to my house. Steve and I were going to see a movie, but since we had a few minutes to kill before the movie started, we stopped by to look at books. I noticed a table stationed right next to the cash registers which was filled with books about the end of time. Books about the battle of Armageddon, the Antichrist and the Y2K computer bug were spread out for all to see. There must have been twenty-five or thirty titles on this table—there was even a millennium clock, which was counting down the days, hours and minutes to January 1, 2000. This date has since come and gone, but end-time prophecy continues to mean big business, big bucks and big sales. Surprisingly, even after the smooth transition from 1999 to 2000, the fever has not subsided.

Because the end of history is a Biblical topic and because the religious culture around us is rife with fanciful theories related to it, there is the need for all serious Bible students to carefully examine the issue. I pray that this volume will serve as a helpful introduction to what is a fascinating and often misunderstood subject.

Millennial Fever

What's All the Fuss About?

Fever Pitch

Concerning the coming of our Lord Jesus Christ and our being gathered to him, we ask you, brothers, not to become easily unsettled or alarmed by some prophecy, report or letter supposed to have come from us, saying that the day of the Lord has already come. Don't let anyone deceive you in any way, for that day will not come until the rebellion occurs and the man of lawlessness is revealed, the man doomed to destruction. He will oppose and will exalt himself over everything that is called God or is worshiped, so that he sets himself up in God's temple, proclaiming himself to be God.

...And then the lawless one will be revealed, whom the Lord Jesus will overthrow with the breath of his mouth and destroy by the splendor of his coming.

2 Thessalonians 2:1-4, 8

The mark of the beast, Armageddon, the Rapture, 666, Gog and Magog, and the Antichrist have become a part of everyday vocabulary. In the religious world, both polls and publishing statistics help show the widespread interest in the end times. For example, a recent Associated Press poll of Christian adults indicated that one out of every four believes that Jesus will return in his or her lifetime—this is an estimated twenty-six million people. An earlier 1988 Gallup poll reported that eighty percent of Americans feel they will appear before God on the Judgment Day. Back in 1977, a survey revealed that there were eight million premillennialists in America. At the beginning of that decade, Hal Lindsey's *The Late Great Planet Earth* was published and has sold more than fifteen million copies. Additionally, the Jehovah's Witnesses have distributed millions of copies of their *Watchtower* publication. In 1987, Logos Bookstore in Los Angeles had no fewer than eighty-one separate prophecy-related books for sale. Today, the same store offers more than 350 different books that address apocalyptic and end-time topics. Furthermore, seminarians can now be trained in prophetic theology at Dallas Theological Seminary or the Moody Bible Institute in Chicago.

However, thoughts about the end of time are not just found among religious thinkers. Secular writers and filmmakers have caught the millennium bug too. On the silver screen *The Omen* trilogy took apocalyptic symbols from the book of Revelation and produced three horror movies—*The Omen* (1976), *Damien: Omen II* (1978) and *The Final Conflict* (1981). Other movies have made use of apocalyptic themes including *Ghostbusters* (1984), *The Seventh Sign* (1988), *The Rapture* (1991) and Steven King's *The Stand* (1994). Chris Carter, creator of my favorite television series of all time, *The X-Files,* took aim at the millennial fever by creating a new show for the Fox Network appropriately titled *Millennium.* Alex Heard's *Apocalypse Pretty Soon: Travels in*

End-Time America and James Finn Garner's *Apocalypse Wow: A Memoir for the End of Time* are but two of the recent flurry of books that lampoon this infatuation with the end of the world. Examples of modern rock groups that have used Biblical apocalyptic symbols in their songs include the Eagles in "Hotel California," Genesis in "Apocalypse in 9/8," and REM in "It's the End of the World As We Know It," to name a few.

Tim LaHaye and Jerry B. Jenkins have coauthored one of the most successful series of novels ever, the *Left Behind* series, which focuses on the rapture, the tribulation and events associated with a premillennial view of the end of time. Written by two evangelicals, the book has crossed over into the secular market and is widely read by those with no previous interest in Biblical topics. According to the authors' Web site, "With the prophetic teachings of the Bible as the background, this dynamic apocalyptic fiction has captured the imaginations of millions."[1]

Millennial fever is all around us.

Coming to Terms

A discussion of end-time prophecy brings with it a number of possibly unfamiliar terms. Before we continue, here is a handy listing of some of them.

Prophecy—To preach, to declare, to foretell, to forth-tell. The classic Hebrew prophets of the eighth and seventh centuries BC were people like you and me who were taken hold of by the Word of Yahweh. Because they had received God's word, they *had* to declare it to the people.

Apocalyptic—*Apokalypto* is a Greek word that means "to reveal what is hidden, to make known." Apocalyptic writing used symbols and metaphors to disclose information to a specific group of people who was usually undergoing persecution and was in need of encouragement.

Eschatology (pronounced "Ess-kuh-TALL-uh-jee")—The study of last things or the end of time, from the Greek word *eschatos*, meaning "last."

Parousia (pronounced "pah-ROO-zee-uh")—The Second Coming of Jesus, from a Greek word meaning "presence or arrival."

Millennium—A period of one thousand years, from two Latin words: *mille*, which means "one thousand" and *annus*, which means "year." Specifically, this term refers to the thousand-year reign of Christ mentioned in Revelation 20.

Chiliasm (pronounced "KILL-ee-iz-um")—From the Greek word *chilioi*, meaning "a thousand." This term is often derogatory and usually applied in place of "millennialism" when describing a particularly sensual or carnal view of the millennium.

Premillennialism—*Pre-* means "before," thus premillennialism teaches that the Parousia will occur before the millennium. After the "Rapture" and the "Tribulation," Jesus will establish a kingdom and rule on earth with the saints for a literal one thousand years. This belief is held by a large number of evangelicals today.

Postmillennialism—*Post-* is a prefix that means "after," so a postmillennialist is one who believes that Jesus will return at the end of the millennium. According to this view, due to Christianity's victorious influence in society, life on earth will gradually become better and better until the millennial kingdom of Christ becomes a reality on the earth, after which Jesus will usher humanity into eternity. This belief was prevalent among theologians in the late nineteenth and early twentieth centuries.

Amillennialism—The prefix *a-* means "not," and accordingly, amillennialism teaches that there is not a literal millennial reign of Jesus on earth associated with the end of time. When Jesus comes to judge the world, time will end and the world will be destroyed.

Does Anybody Really Know What Time It Is?

Y2K—the year 2000—has a magical ring to it. But did it actually mark the dawn of the new millennium? Although most people believe that January 1, 2000, began the third millennium AD, they don't understand the errors that have been made in the calendar over the past two thousand years. Did January 1, 2000, begin the new millennium? Check this out.

Around 525 AD, a Roman monk named Dionysius Exiguus, whose name means "Dennis the Short," began to propose that the Christian era should begin with the nativity, or birth of Jesus. He set the birth of Jesus as the year one "AD," which is Latin for *anno Domini*—"in the year of our Lord."

Therefore, the "Christian" calendar did not begin with January 1, 0000, but with January 1, 0001. Thus, the third millennium would actually begin on January 1, 2001, making the year 2000 the last year of the twentieth century, not the first year of the twenty-first century! Dennis the Short was a year "short" when he proposed his calendar. (This is the kind of stuff that "inquiring minds" want to know!)

If this were not confusing enough, the new dating system suggested by Dionysius was not adopted with regularity until about two hundred years after his suggestion. Historians give credit to Bede (c. 673-735 AD), the English scholar and historian, for standardizing the acceptance of this new way of calculating dates. Some time later, scholars began to notice a discrepancy between calendar time and solar time. Calendar time (365 days) was slightly shorter than solar time (365 days, 5 hours, 48 minutes and 46 seconds). So, in 1582, Pope Gregory XIII issued a calendar reform to fix this discrepancy. People went to bed on October 4, 1852, to wake up the next morning and discover it was now October 15—yes, eleven days had been added to the calendar! (This gives the one-hour jump in Daylight Savings Time new meaning!) In addition, the "leap year" was instituted to keep the Gregorian calendar in sync with solar time.

If you still aren't confused yet, there is more. Recently, scholars have discovered that Dionysius was in error when he calculated the year of Jesus' birth. We know that Jesus was born while Herod the Great was still alive (Matthew 2:1), and scholars now date the death of Herod around 4 BC. This would place the birth of Jesus somewhere between 6-4 BC. Yes, Jesus was born BC or "before Christ"!

Therefore, the 2000-year anniversary of the birth of Jesus occurred sometime between 1994 and 1996. And if you remove from the calendar the eleven days that Gregory XIII inserted in 1582, then January 1 actually comes on December 21.

It would seem that the third millennium began while no one was looking! Does anybody really know what time it is?

How Long, to Sing This Song?

End-Time Prophecy in Church History

Apocalyptic soothsayers have always had a good foundation upon which to base their writings—the Bible. From the middle of the second century BC through the first century AD, a genre of religious literature known as apocalyptic writing flourished in Judaism, usually bearing a strong resemblance to elements of the book of Daniel. The term "apocalyptic" comes from the Greek word *apokalypsis* meaning "revelation" or "unveiling." The identifying feature of these Jewish apocalyptic works was the recounting of visions as the vehicle for relating a prophetic message. And as they were nearly always written in the context of opposition and persecution, the use of symbols played a predominant role in communicating God's ultimate victory over the enemies of his persecuted people.

The Old Testament (OT) books of Daniel and Ezekiel contain early examples of apocalyptic writing. Other books referred to as the "Apocrypha"—written for the most part in the period of time between the writing of the Old and New Testaments and not usually held to be part of the canon of Scripture—contain many examples of apocalyptic writing, such as *IV Esdras* and *Bel and the Dragon*. In fact, the Jews of the intertestamental period spawned quite a few apocalyptic works—as many as seventy of them! In the New Testament, Mark 13, Matthew 24, Luke 21 and the book of Revelation are all examples of apocalyptic writing.

End-Time Prophecy and the Early Church

With these examples of apocalyptic symbolism circulating in the first century, how did the early church view the end of time? They believed they were living in the last days. Yet they were not obsessed with the imminent establishment of an earthly millennial kingdom. They believed that the church *was* the kingdom of God and that at the proper time—God's time—God would send Jesus back to the earth to end time and judge the world.

The first century church was heavily persecuted by Rome. As those persecutions intensified under Nero (around 65 AD), apocalyptic writers began to make symbolic references about the victory that the Christians would have if they stayed faithful to the cause. The gospel writers included the short apocalyptic sections of Jesus' teaching in their Gospels to help fortify the faith of persecuted Christians. Toward the end of the first century, possibly during the reign of the Emperor Vespasian (69-79 AD),

the apostle John received an apocalyptic vision concerni'
impending persecution of Christians in the first century. ...
book of Revelation contains this vision and was written to let the
Christians know that at the end of the battle, when all was said
and done, Christ and his church would be victorious over
Domitian and the Roman Empire. The Christians should not lose
hope, for in the end, God would win.

Church leaders from the first few centuries of Christianity
whose writings we possess—often referred to as the early church
fathers—did not have much to say concerning the end of time.
Their writings contain only a few short phrases on the topic. For
example, Papias (c. 60-130 AD) believed in a millennial kingdom
of Christ upon the earth. He did not attempt to say when this
kingdom would materialize, but he did envision it as a time when
Christ would personally rule over a golden age on the earth.

Around 170 AD, a Phrygian religious leader named Montanus
arrived on the scene who proclaimed that he was the Holy Spirit
incarnate. He prophesied that the Final Judgment was imminent
and that God would establish an earthly kingdom, the New
Jerusalem, in Phrygia. His followers were called Montanists.
They practiced asceticism, separating themselves from the world
to prepare for the coming kingdom of Christ. They spread his
teachings throughout North Africa, the Middle East and parts of
Europe.

The early church denounced the teachings of Montanus as
false teachings, and Montanus was proclaimed a heretic. Irenaeus
(c. 130 - 200 AD) wrote a treatise entitled *Against Heresies* in which

he debunked Montanus' teachings. Irenaeus surveyed the Biblical apocalypses in his writing. He concluded that when Jesus came again, he would establish a kingdom on the earth that would last one thousand years. After this time, the world would be judged and time would be no more.

End–Time Prophecy After 325 AD

When Christianity became the state religion during the rule of the Emperor Constantine in 325 AD, the teaching of the church became codified under the influence of church councils. The leading theologian during this time was Augustine (354-430 AD), and his teaching was not strongly futuristic. He believed in a last judgment in which Jesus would come to separate the good from the bad. This would be the end of time. The views of Augustine became orthodoxy and held the field for several centuries.

As the year 1000 AD approached, speculation about the end of time began to rise. It is difficult to determine how much of a sensation the approaching new millennium caused; scholars are divided on this point. We do know that during the Middle Ages, several apocalyptic writings were generated and disseminated among the population of Europe. The Sibylline oracles, a collection of verse "prophecies" about the end of time, were being circulated. Hildegard of Bingen, a twelfth-century German mystic, wrote about her vision of the Antichrist and the end of the world. (See the shaded box in this chapter for a discussion of the Biblical use of "antichrist.") The visions of Daniel and Revelation gripped the medieval mind.

Pick the Antichrist!

Dear children, this is the last hour; and as you have heard that the antichrist is coming, even now many antichrists have come. This is how we know it is the last hour. (1 John 2:18)

Who is the liar? It is the man who denies that Jesus is the Christ. Such a man is the antichrist—he denies the Father and the Son. (1 John 2:22)

Every spirit that does not acknowledge Jesus is not from God. This is the spirit of the antichrist, which you have heard is coming and even now is already in the world. (1 John 4:3)

Many deceivers, who do not acknowledge Jesus Christ as coming in the flesh, have gone out into the world. Any such person is the deceiver and the antichrist. (2 John 1:7)

The idea of a personal "Antichrist" who will somehow embody the forces of evil at the end of time is a popularly held view today. Scripturally, however, there is little basis for this view. The only occurrences of the word "antichrist" in the entire Bible (cited above) appear in two letters of the apostle John. Even a cursory reading of these verses brings to light at least three discrepancies with today's Hollywood version.

First, John was referring to anti-Christian forces that were already at work in the first century. End-time prognosticators are mistaken about *when* the activity of the antichrist would occur.

Second, there is no indication that this title was ever meant to apply to a lone, specific individual. Rather, "many" deceivers are referred to as "antichrists." Predictors of the end-time are mistaken about *how many* antichrists are referred to in Scripture.

Third, those who were considered by John to be antichrists were false teachers who were spreading wrong views about the nature of Christ. The one to be seriously dreaded was not some sort of powerful persecutor, but rather, a deceiver who could undermine the foundations of Christianity with false teachings about Jesus. End-time prognosticators are mistaken about *the nature* of the threat of the antichrist.

In spite of the obvious problems that arise when such a view is exposed to an open Bible, the suggestion that John had a particular individual in mind has been around for a long time. In this part of the book, you get to meet a number of people whose contemporaries have honored them with the title of "the Antichrist." Were they correct? If you miss, that's okay. Many have missed before you!

Here are some of the more prominent candidates that have been put forward.

Nero
Domitian
Frederick II
Hohenstaufen
Muhammed
Attila the Hun
The Pope
(throughout the centuries)
Saladin
Martin Luther
Charles I
The kings/queens of England
(during the American Revolution)
Napoleon Bonaparte
Benito Mussolini
Adolf Hitler
Franklin Delano Roosevelt
Francisco Franco
Mikhail Gorbachev
A Euro-Common Market Computer
John F. Kennedy
Anwar Sadat
Henry Kissinger
Ronald Reagan
Sun Myung Moon
Saddam Hussein

The most celebrated apocalypticist of the Middle Ages was Joachim of Fiore (c. 1135-1202). After several years of concentrated study on the book of Revelation, he published his *Exposition on Revelation*. He saw the world in three dispensations—the period of Law, ruled over by God the Father; the period of Grace, overseen by the Son; and the period of the Spirit, a time which would follow the tribulation in which the Spirit would rule over the righteous. This breaking of history into dispensations would greatly influence Protestant writers in Britain and America in the nineteenth and twentieth centuries and would become the foundation of premillennial dispensationalism.

Protestant End-Time Prophecy

The year 1517 would witness the dawn of a new age as Luther nailed his ninety-five theses to the door of the Wittenburg Castle church, signaling the beginning of the Protestant Reformation. The teachings of Luther, Zwingli and Calvin would shape the Protestant reform churches for the next two hundred years. This was true of the Protestant view of end-time prophecy. Hearkening back to Augustine, Luther, Zwingli and Calvin were typically amillennial in their approach. Therefore, any Protestant group that taught a different view of the end of time became a fringe group and was regarded with suspicion.

This is true of Thomas Müntzer who became the leading religious spokesman of the Peasant War in the 1520s in Germany. Müntzer believed that an apocalyptic war was beginning which would rid the world of evil and usher in a kingdom of God upon the earth. He sided with the peasants and against Martin Luther and the German princes in this war, believing that the Holy Spirit revealed his will directly to true Christians and that God was on the side of the peasants. The peasants began to look for the return of Christ, hoping that this would deliver them from harm. Instead, some 5,000 rebels were slaughtered, and Müntzer was beheaded on May 15, 1525. Some estimate that as many as 100,000 people were killed during the Peasant War of 1524-25.

In the 1530s the Anabaptists began to stir in Germany and Europe. The name Anabaptist was given to them by their opponents but comes from their belief in adult baptism. These separatists did not accept the union of Luther with the German nobility or the ideals of Calvin's theocracy in Geneva. They stressed a personal piety, nonresistance to evil and violence, and a separation from the world. They became strong in Switzerland and the Netherlands. Some Anabaptists believed that Christ and the Antichrist had already begun to battle over the fate of the earth and that the end of the world was near. Under John of Leiden, a radical group of Anabaptists took control of the city of Münster, Westphalia, declaring it to be the New Jerusalem. The city was recaptured in 1535 by an army raised by German princes, and the leaders were tortured and killed. The persecution of Anabaptists— by Protestants and Catholics alike—increased throughout Europe with little effort made to distinguish between the belligerent minority and the pacifist majority. Such persecution added fuel to the apocalyptic fervor of the Anabaptists.

End-Time Americana

As the United States was drafting its constitution, religious leaders in the young nation were touting it as the New Jerusalem: the answer to prophetic projections of Daniel, Ezekiel and the apostle John. Some writers claimed that England was the Army from the North described in Revelation. They interpreted the king of England to be the Antichrist. They saw the struggle to launch the new nation as the dawn of a new millennium. The early political figures in America believed they were creating a New World based upon a new standard of equality, liberty and a pursuit of happiness for each individual. They proclaimed that theirs was the land flowing with milk and honey.

Although other views circulated in America, prominent preachers like Jonathan Edwards (1703-58) believed that the progress of human history had been moving continuously forward, that the kingdom of God was coming ever closer, and that a spiritual awakening in America could lead directly to the establishment of a millennial kingdom of Jesus on the earth. The Second Coming would occur at the close of this millennial age as its crowning event. Edwards's postmillennial views carried the day for theologians in America for the next hundred and fifty years.

Liberal preachers like Walter Rauschenbush took up the theme of postmillennialism, with its optimistic view of human history, and married it with humanism from Europe. Based in Rochester, New York, he preached a social gospel, claiming that the foremost call of Christianity was to help the poor. In doing so, Christians could usher in the kingdom of God. The City of God, it was often thought, would be in America. This idealistic optimism would flourish until it was dashed to the rocks with two world wars in the early 1900s.

Of interest to some will be the fact that the two leaders of the Stone-Campbell Restoration Movement had different views about the millennium. Alexander Campbell was a wealthy and prominent American who was instrumental in starting the Disciples of

Christ/Churches of Christ (Campbellites). In the 1820s he em-
braced the Second Coming of Jesus as a central tenet of his
preaching. He began a journal called *The Millennial Harbinger*,
and his thinking was predominantly postmillennial. He believed
that the restoration of true Christianity throughout the cities of
America might very well be preparing the way for Christ to return.
Barton Stone, on the other hand, was decidedly premillennial in
outlook. His followers had a more otherworldly and countercultural
view, believing that society would be changed only when Christ
returned and established his millennial reign. In spite of their
disagreement about the end times, they managed to maintain
unity in the early decades of their movement.

End-Times: Premillennial Dispensational Style

One of the most well-known early proponents of premillennial
doctrine in America was William Miller. Miller was a farmer from
upstate New York and a Baptist layman. Through his study of
prophecy he concluded that the Lord would return in the year
1843. As 1843 began, he clarified that the end would come
sometime between March 21, 1843, and March 21, 1844. Many
thousands of Millerites passed out tracts that heralded the Lord's
return, left their fields unplowed, and quit jobs and businesses to
spread the word and to prepare for the end. When the forecasted
date came and went, the "First Disappointment" was followed up
with a recalculation of October 22, 1844, as the last day. A similar
frenzy ensued until the "Great Disappointment" of October 22,
1844, left Millerites in disarray and bitterly divided. The movement

failed soon thereafter, but the predictions did not end. Millerites James and Ellen G. White began the Seventh Day Adventist church, and other religious leaders studied the prophecies of Daniel and Revelation to come up with their own elaborate systems of determining when Jesus would return to the earth. This was Miller's legacy to the premillennial debate.

A British preacher, John Nelson Darby (1800-1882), is considered by many to be the father of premillennial dispensationalism. He joined a group called the Plymouth Brethren in the 1840s. Darby expounded the concept that God had spoken to humanity in various ways throughout history. The various periods in which God communicated with humanity could be called "dispensations," and in each dispensation, God's means of saving humanity was different. According to Darby, the present dispensation—the Church Age—is a parenthesis in history. Bible prophecy is silent during this age, which is simply a prelude to the next golden age that will lead to the end of the world. At present we are waiting for the Rapture, a time when Jesus will call all the saved to be with him in heaven. Those left behind will face a seven-year period that will see the rise of the Antichrist, the Apostate Church and the Tribulation. This time of tribulation will end with the Battle of Armageddon and the triumph of Jesus who will then begin his millennial reign upon the earth.

Does all of this sound familiar? Premillennial dispensationalism has many forms and varieties, but nearly all of it is based on the teaching of J. N. Darby. Not only did his teaching influence William Miller and the Seventh Day Adventists, Charles Taze Russell and the Jehovah's Witnesses and Herbert Armstrong's Worldwide Church of God, but many evangelical churches as well. The themes can be thoroughly explored in the notes of the Scofield Reference Bible, which was produced by Cyrus I. Scofield (1843-1921). Scofield, who was influenced by the ministry of Dwight L. Moody, became the pastor of the Dallas First Congregational Church in 1882 and printed his annotated Bible in 1909. *The Scofield Reference Bible* has done more to unify and disseminate premillennial doctrine than any other work. By putting Darby's system in the notes of the Bible, many people came to accept premillennial dispensationalism without question.

When Scofield left Dallas, he was succeeded by his friend Lewis Sperry Chafer, who founded the Dallas Theological Seminary in 1924. As the institutional home of premillennial dispensationalism, the faculty has included several big names in this school of thought, including John F. Walvoord (author of *The Rapture Question: Armageddon, Oil, and the Middle East Crisis*), J. Dwight Pentecost (*Prophecy for Today*), and Charles C. Ryrie (*The Ryrie Study Bible, What You Should Know About the Rapture*). Perhaps the most well-known graduate of the seminary is Hal Lindsey, whose *The Late Great Planet Earth*, published in 1970, was called the "no. 1 nonfiction best-seller of the decade" by *The New York Times*.

N

Where are things at today? At present, postmillennialism is almost dead; a few religious groups and some liberal denominations hold to this view of the end of time. Catholic churches and most traditional Protestant denominations, if they have a stated doctrine, are usually amillennial. The majority of evangelical churches, however, currently hold to a premillennial view of the last days, with dispensationalism having the loudest advocates.

Premillennialism Explained

Investigating What Is Being Taught

Three Millennial Theories

Prophecy interpreters, like hobbyists assembling a picture puzzle or artisans crafting a mosaic, painstakingly build from hundreds of Bible verses a picture of the final days of human history—a picture strikingly similar to the world of today.

Paul Boyer, author of When Time Shall Be No More

We believe whatever we want to believe.

Demosthenes, philosopher

What will happen when Jesus returns to the earth? The belief that he will return is an undisputed tenet of the Christian faith. But how he will return and the events surrounding his Second Coming have been understood in a number of different ways. These differences have to do primarily with the relationship between his Second Advent and the reign of one thousand years that is mentioned in only one place in the Bible: Revelation chapter 20. Three ways of looking at this relationship have given rise to the three most common schools of thought in the Biblical study of last things. Having briefly defined them earlier, we will now examine each in more detail.

Amillennialism

Amillennialists teach that there will be no literal earthly millennial kingdom of Jesus. When Jesus returns, he comes to judge the living and the dead, bring time to a close, usher in eternity and destroy the world. Amillennialists believe that Jesus' kingdom is already present on the earth because they believe that part of Jesus' mission was to establish a spiritual kingdom. Therefore, when the church was established on the day of Pentecost in Acts 2, the kingdom arrived on earth that same day.

Amillennialists believe that many of the prophecies used by premillennialists to describe the end of time have already been fulfilled. Accordingly, when Daniel 2 prophesies about the coming kingdom of God being established during the age of the Roman Empire, this prophecy is seen to be speaking of God's church. Amillennialists hold that Mark 13 and Matthew 24 are prophesying, for the most part, about the destruction of the temple in Jerusalem. And Revelation is interpreted in its historical context to show that it was written to help the Christians of the first century get ready for persecution that would come their way, probably during the reign of the Roman Emperor Domitian.[1] Therefore, the binding of Satan and the millennium described in

Revelation 20 are not to be understood literally, but as metaphorically depicting what is happening now—in the church age. Amillennialists primarily take this position because they believe it is the most consistent with all other references to the Parousia, or Second Coming, found in the New Testament.

Postmillennialism

Postmillennialists have several points in common with amillennialists. They believe that Christians are now in the kingdom of God. As members of God's kingdom, we are to preach the good news of Jesus to the world. The more we preach and practice Christianity, the better the world will become. It is in their optimistic view of human history and progress that the postmillenialists differ most from the other views. They believe that we are progressing toward a better tomorrow, in large part due to the active presence of the church of Jesus in this world. At some point in the future, hopefully sooner and not later, the world will accept Christianity and the millennial kingdom of Christ will come into the world. This earthly millennial kingdom will be the dawn of a Golden Age upon the earth, when humanity will live at peace with each other and with the earth. The following passage has been thought to describe this Golden Age, and some have taken it as a literal description of the millennium.

> The wolf will live with the lamb,
> the leopard will lie down with the goat,
> the calf and the lion and the yearling together;
> and a little child will lead them.

The cow will feed with the bear,
   their young will lie down together,
   and the lion will eat straw like the ox.
The infant will play near the hole of the cobra,
   and the young child put his hand into the viper's nest.
They will neither harm nor destroy
   on all my holy mountain,
for the earth will be full of the knowledge of the LORD
   as the waters cover the sea. (Isaiah 11:6-9)

The wolf and the lamb will lie down with each other; there will be no war, no pollution, no sickness, no hunger, no poverty and no crime and sin will be totally eliminated. Christ will rule over all his creation. Everyone will accept the precepts of Christianity.

Postmillenialists hold that the one thousand years described in Revelation 20 may or may not be a literal one thousand years. If literal, it will be difficult to determine when this thousand-year period begins, because it will be a process that will evolve over time. The millennial kingdom will arrive in degrees, not in a sudden storm, and at the end of the thousand years, Jesus will raise and judge the dead. Everyone will go into their final place in eternity—heaven for the righteous and hell for the unrighteous.

But is the world truly getting better and better? Violent wars and social decay in the twentieth century have "cured" most postmillenialists of such optimism. More importantly, does Scripture teach such an outlook of history? Consider what Jesus had to say in these verses:

"Enter through the narrow gate. For wide is the gate and broad is the road that leads to destruction, and many enter through it. But small is the gate and narrow the road that leads to life, and only a few find it." (Matthew 7:13-14)

"Because of the increase of wickedness, the love of most will grow cold." (Matthew 24:12)

"However, when the Son of Man comes, will he find faith on the earth?" (Luke 18:8)

C. S. Lewis, author and literary critic, offers this criticism of postmillennialism:

The doctrine of the Second Coming is deeply uncongenial to the whole evolutionary or developmental character of modern thought. We have been taught to think of the world as something that grows slowly towards perfection, something that "progresses" or "evolves." Christian Apocalyptic offers us no such hope. It does not even foretell (which would be more tolerable to our habits of thought) a gradual decay. It foretells a sudden, violent end imposed from without; an extinguisher popped onto the candle, a brick flung at the gramophone, a curtain rung down on the play—"Halt!"[2]

Premillennialism

Premillennialism is the belief, as the name implies, that Jesus will return to the earth before inaugurating a literal thousand-year reign. Today over eight million evangelicals are premillennialists. Most denominational Christian television shows like "The 700 Club" hold a premillennial point of view. Ministers like Hal

Lindsey, Grant R. Jeffery and John Hagee have sold hundreds of thousands of books expounding this doctrine. The most apparent characteristic of today's premillennial doctrine is the use of prophetic/apocalyptic scripture to define signs of the end of time. Images are taken from Daniel, Ezekiel, Malachi, Mark 13, 1 Thessalonians 4, Revelation and other passages. These scriptures are interpreted as describing what is going on in the world today. Most of these scriptures are separated from the historical situation in which they were written and applied to the present. Premillennialists take a dash of Daniel, a pinch of Ezekiel, a touch of Thessalonians and a huge helping of Revelation; then they pitch them into a cauldron of prophetic end-time prophecy and stir until well done.

Since this view is so prevalent in mainstream Christianity today, we will devote the next chapter to exploring what premillennialism teaches, in particular the modern brand of the doctrine known as dispensational premillennialism.

Dispensational Premillennialism

The Short Course

What is taught in premillennial circles today? Before you can understand a typical dispensationalist scenario of the end of the world, you must become familiar with some of the end-time jargon of premillennialism.

Rapture—A word that is not found in the Bible. It comes from the Latin *rapiemur*, which means "caught up." In 1 Thessalonians 4:17, Paul describes how those who are still alive at the Lord's coming will be "caught up" to meet Jesus in the air.

Pre-Rapture—Signs that begin to signal the coming Rapture of the church.

The Remnant—Those not lucky or not righteous enough to meet Jesus in the air during the Rapture must now face the Tribulation.

The Antichrist—A personal embodiment of the forces of evil. The Antichrist will enter the scene soon after the Rapture to form a one-world government, a one-world cashless economy, and a one-world religion. (See the box in chapter 2 for a discussion of the Biblical usage of "antichrist.")

The Tribulation—A period of intense suffering and hardship that will last for seven years. It will witness the rise of the Antichrist, the conversion of Israel to Christianity and the epic battle of Armageddon.

Armageddon—A great battle to be held at the close of the Tribulation in which the Messiah will return to lead an army of the saints against the army of the Antichrist. The Messiah will triumph in this battle.

The Millennium—After the battle of Armageddon, Jesus will rule on the earth for a thousand years with his saints. Satan will be "bound" and his activities severely curtailed during this reign of the righteous on the earth.

The Last Judgment—After the Millennium, the world will face final judgment.

The defining end-time moment for premillennialists is the Rapture. This is the instant in which Jesus will come back to the earth to stealthily whisk all the righteous to heaven. Those who remain on the earth will live through a seven-year period called the Tribulation. Events immediately preceding the Rapture are thus part of the "pre-Tribulation," the signs of the end of the age.

The ABCs of Dispensationalism

The premillennial view of the end of time has been around since the early centuries of Christianity. However, beginning in the nineteenth century, a peculiar school of premillennial thought arrived on the scene with the introduction of a theological perspective known as dispensationalism. Although dispensational premillennialism (what a mouthful!) has little in common with earlier forms, it has come to dominate the "premill" landscape. Today's most prominent premillennialists are nearly all dispensational in their outlook.

What is dispensationalism, and how has it influenced thinking about end-time prophecy? And what, if anything, is wrong with this approach?

WHAT'S THAT YOU SAY?	WHAT'S WRONG WITH THAT?
As the name implies, dispensationalism lumps time into seven unequal periods—called *dispensations* or *economies*—in which God has dealt with man in distinctive ways.[1] Scripture is "rightly divided"[2] such that "five of these dispensations, or periods of time, have been fulfilled; we are living in the sixth, probably toward its close, and have before us the seventh, and last: the millennium."[3]	Any attempt to interpret Scripture must recognize the differences in God's dealings with mankind according to his various covenants. However, the rigid approach taken by dispensationalism artificially chops the Bible into segments, and it fails to account for the continuity of God's character of grace throughout the Old and New Testaments.
A permanent distinction is made between Israel and the church, such that God's promises made to Israel are seen as eternally separate from his promises made to the church. So, his promises to Israel must find their fulfillment in a future Tribulation and Millennium, not in the church established by Jesus Christ.	Certainly, Israel as a national entity is distinct from the church. However, God does not maintain a separate plan for ethnic Israel than he does for the rest of humanity. Salvation today is the same for Jew and Gentile alike, entailing faithful obedience to Jesus Christ as the sole condition of salvation (Galatians 3:26-29, Hebrews 8:5-13,

	1 Peter 2:9-10). The church of Christ constitutes his chosen people today. Dispensationalists minimize the significance of Jesus' *first* coming and the role of his church.
The hermeneutic applied to all Scripture, regardless of genre, is "literal, except when embarrassing."[4]	Applying a literal interpretation to the symbolism of apocalyptic literature *ought* to be embarrassing. This approach has led to a lot of "majoring in the minors," and many "experts" have gone into great detail about the particulars of their end-time system. Moreover, current events are arbitrarily designated as fulfillments of prophecy in a way that only inspired men could possibly claim to know.

Notes

1. The seven dispensations are: Innocence (from Creation to the Fall, Genesis 1:26-3:24); Conscience (from the Fall to the Flood, Genesis 4:1-7:24); Human Government (from the Flood to Abram, Genesis 8:1-11:26); Promise (from Abram to the giving of the Law on Sinai, Genesis 11:27-Exodus 18); Law (from Sinai to the Cross, Exodus 19:1-Acts 1:26); Grace (from the death of Christ to the judgments in Revelation, Acts 2:1-Revelation 19:21); and Kingdom (Christ's millennial reign, Revelation 20:1-22:21).

2. 2 Timothy 2:15 KJV.

3. C. I. Scofield, *Rightly Dividing the Word of Truth* (Neptune, New Jersey: Loizeaux Bros., 1986; First edition, 1896), 13-14.

4. Michael Gilstrap, in the newsletter *Dispensationalism in Transition* (Tyler, Texas: Institute for Christian Economics) Vol. 1, No. 5, May, 1988.

After the seven years of Tribulation, Jesus will establish his millennial kingdom on the earth.

The concept of the Rapture becomes even more convoluted due to the failure of premillennialists to agree upon when it will take place. Some say it will happen just before the Tribulation begins (pre-Tribulation Rapture), some say it will come three-and-a-half years into the Tribulation (mid-Tribulation Rapture), and some say it will occur at the end of the Tribulation (post-Tribulation Rapture). It seems that premillennialists have quite a fixation on the "Rapture," a word that never even occurs in the Bible—not once, nada, never.

Today's premillennialists go into great detail about the succession of events that will unfold at the end of the age. What will occur during the pre-Rapture/pre-Tribulation time? What will be the signs of the end-time? There will be false messiahs and wars (Matthew 24:4-6). There will be famine, pestilence and earthquakes (Matthew 24:7-8). According to Ezekiel 37-39, the Jews must return to their homeland in Israel. Many evangelical premillennialists were overjoyed when the United Nations declared Israel a state in 1948. They saw this as a direct fulfillment of OT prophecy. They continue to support the State of Israel today because they believe Israel must continue to occupy Palestine in order for the Lord to return.

But premillennialists do not stop there. They declare that the Jews must occupy the Old City of Jerusalem. The Jews must rebuild the temple of God on the Temple Mount inside the Old City of Jerusalem. This must occur in order for the Abomination of Desolation (a profaning of the altar of sacrifice) to occur. This was prophesied in Daniel 9:27 and Matthew 24:15. Temple worship and temple sacrifices must begin anew.

Today the Arabs occupy most of the Old City of Jerusalem. The Arabs control the Temple Mount. It is the third holiest site in

Signs of the Times

Events that have been hailed by premillennialists as pre-Rapture signs:

- The Great War of 1914-1918 (World War I)
- The formation of the League of Nations
- The return of Jews to Palestine
- The atheistic arrogance of Soviet dictators
- The formation of the European Common Market
- The alliance of Mussolini and Hitler
- The development of atomic weapons

- The creation of the Jewish State of Israel in 1948
- Y2K—the computer bug
- The Arab confederation solidified against the state of Israel
- The rise of a great military force in Red China with millions of soldiers
- Increase in wars, earthquakes, famines, pestilence and pollution
- The "New World Order" of the post-Cold War era
- The rise of credit cards, computer banking and a cashless society

Islam. The Al-Aksa Mosque and the Dome of the Rock stand on the Temple Mount. Every Friday, thousands of Muslims flood into the Temple Mount to worship. Premillennialists believe that all this must stop. They find themselves siding with the Jews and against the Arabs in conflicts over Jerusalem. They support Jewish institutions like the Temple Institute which study how the temple can be rebuilt today. They are pro-Israel because they believe prophecies about Israel must be fulfilled before Jesus will return.

As Israel gets stronger and prepares to rebuild the temple, an Army from the North will begin to assemble to confront Israel. Ezekiel 38-39, Daniel 11:40-45 and Joel 2:20 prophesy about this army. While this army has been identified in various ways throughout history, most recently premillennialists have focused on the Soviet Union and the communist bloc countries as being the Army of the North. With the collapse of the Soviet Union, premillennialists have redirected these prophecies toward a confederation of countries surrounding Russia.

The King of the South will join forces with the Army of the North (Daniel 11:42-43, Ezekiel 30:4-5). Most interpret the King of the South as being a leader of the Arab states headed by Egypt. To the surprise of all (except those initiated few that understand end-time prophecy), Israel defeats the Army of the North (Ezekiel 38:15ff.). Then comes the Rapture, if you believe in a pre-Tribulation Rapture, that is. The righteous will be taken up in the air to meet Jesus (1 Thessalonians 4:13-15). Those who are driving will be taken right out of their automobiles. Those asleep will leave from their beds. Airplane pilots will leave in midair. The aftermath will be devastating. Traffic jams will be common as abandoned cars litter the streets. Not one child will be left on the earth. Parents "left behind" will be heartbroken. Elementary schools will cease to exist. Governments will be in disarray. Those left behind will start a mad search for who is left and who has been taken up.

Immediately after the Rapture, a political figure will emerge who promises to lead the world through the chaotic aftermath. This charismatic figure will sign a pact with Israel to give the Jews freedom to worship on the Temple Mount (Daniel 9:21). Those left behind will be drawn to this charismatic leader. He will lead a revived Roman Empire after the prophecy of Daniel (Daniel 2:31-34). Those who have begun to learn about the prophecies of the Bible and follow Jesus will recognize that this leader is the

Antichrist. They will attempt to teach people about the Antichrist and to oppose him.

Three and one-half years into the Tribulation, the Antichrist will break his covenant with Israel. He will desecrate the temple by offering the abomination of desolation on the sacrificial altar (Daniel 9:27, 2 Thessalonians 2:4). The Antichrist will persecute those who opposed him. Christians will suffer greatly during this time. Those who believe in the pre-Tribulation Rapture and the mid-Tribulation Rapture believe that the church will escape this intense persecution. During this last half of the Tribulation, the seven bowls of judgment from Revelation will be emptied on the world (Revelation 15-16), causing half of the world will die.

At the end of the seven years of tribulation, Jesus will return to lead an army against a combined Army of the North, South and East. Most premillennialists believe the Eastern Army to be the millions of foot soldiers available in China. This final battle will be fought on the plains of Meggido, at a mountain called Har Meggido in Hebrew or Armageddon in English (Revelation 16:16). Jesus and his army will defeat the Antichrist and his false prophet. Satan will be bound and the millennial kingdom of Jesus will begin on the earth.

This millennial kingdom will last one thousand years. During this time, Jesus will rule his people on the earth. At the end of this one-thousand-year period, Satan will be released to wage war against the saints for one last time. After a time of persecution, Jesus will call an end to the war and banish Satan to hell for eternity. The world will now be judged—the righteous will go to heaven and the unrighteous to hell. Eternity begins.

N

As an overview of modern premillennialism, the foregoing description does not take into account all of the minor variations and prognostications that are a part of the current premillennial landscape. It does however represent a fairly accurate picture of dispensational premillennialism as popularly taught in many evangelical churches today. To be sure, all of this makes for some interesting reading; but does it really do justice to the Bible, to the historical context of these passages, and to contemporary and historical events? These are questions we shall explore in the chapters that follow.

What's Wrong with This Picture?

Why I Am Not a Premillennialist

Premillennialism is an interesting, dramatic and seemingly cohesive doctrine. Many people are drawn to it because it is so colorful. The thought of a final battle on the plains of Meggido, with Jesus and his army fighting against the three combined armies of the Antichrist, is full of drama. But in the end premillennialism falls short. It does not "rightly divide" the Scriptures that speak of the end of time. What is wrong with premillennialism?

History 101

> I tell you the truth, this generation will certainly not pass away until all these things have happened. (Matthew 24:34)

Hermeneutics, from the Greek word *hermeneuo* meaning "to interpret or explain," is the study of principles for interpreting texts.

It doesn't take a fancy word, however, to know that factors such as historical setting, context and literary genre affect the way a given text or passage should be understood. The prophecies of Ezekiel, Daniel and Zechariah were written for a particular audience in a specific historical setting. Ezekiel prophesied to the Jews exiled to Babylon from Judah. When he spoke to them, his prophecy had specific meaning for the time and place of its hearers. Premillennialists fail to see this. They take prophecy out of its historical setting and attempt to apply it to a twentieth or twenty-first century context. This is not being true to the spirit of prophecy.

This is especially true of premillennialists in their interpretation of the small apocalyptic sections of the Gospels (Matthew 24, Mark 13 and Luke 21). In these passages, Jesus is answering a direct question posed by his first century audience—they want to know when the temple will be destroyed. Premillennialists completely ignore the question that was asked, thus ignoring the context. Instead, they apply the signs in these verses to the end of time. This is sloppy hermeneutics.

When we interpret prophecy, we must first ask, What did prophecy mean to the people who heard it with their own ears? For example, what did the prophecy of Ezekiel mean to the exiled Jews in Babylon? And what did the image of Daniel 2 mean to Nebuchadnezzar as he heard Daniel explain it? And what did the prophecy of Jesus in Mark 13 mean to the first century disciples? And what did the Revelation of John mean to the early church? Beginning with these questions helps us to understand that most prophecy was written to a specific audience that saw it fulfilled in their own generation. Premillennialism fails to understand this dynamic of Biblical prophecy.

Hit and Run Exegesis

One maxim of Biblical interpretation is that a proof text taken out of context is a pretext. Premillennial doctrine is built on pretext, not context. Premillennialists jump from prophecy to prophecy like a barefoot child skipping on hot asphalt in the summer. They barely touch down in Daniel and then they jump to Revelation. As soon as they land in Revelation they are off to Ezekiel. They quickly move from Ezekiel to Matthew 24 and then touch down in 1 Thessalonians 4. With this type of hit and run exegesis, you can never understand what any single passage is trying to say.

I followed one author as he attempted to show that Russia was the land of Magog in the book of Revelation. He jumped from Ezekiel 38 to Ezekiel 1 to Ezekiel 37 to Zechariah 12 to Revelation 20 to Revelation 16, back to Revelation 20 to Genesis 10 to Daniel 9 to Luke 19 and back to Ezekiel 38. Not in one single jump did the author attempt to show a contextual link back to Ezekiel 38. The scriptures were merely launching points for speaking about the end of time. This type of haphazard, slipshod exegesis could be used to predict almost anything.

It seems that what premillennialists are attempting is a sort of hermeneutical slight of hand. A magician "pulls off" his or her magic tricks by distracting the audience just long enough to make the trick work. Premillennialists send the listener through a whirlwind of Biblical passages that daze, confound and confuse the listener. After enough scriptures are referred to, the speaker or writer can draw whatever conclusion he or she desires because the listener is sitting in astonishment at the barrage of passages. In the end, not one passage has been explained in its historical-cultural setting. This type of hermeneutics insults the integrity of the Bible.

Literary Genres

> The sun will be turned to darkness
>   and the moon to blood
>   before the coming of the great and dreadful day of
>   the Lord. (Joel 2:31)

Another characteristic of dispensationalism is its adherence to a literal interpretation of Scriptures. There is a difference, however, between taking the Bible *literally* and taking it *seriously.* A serious student of the Bible realizes that when Jesus said, "If your hand causes you to sin, cut it off" and "If your eye causes you to sin, pluck it out" (Mark 9:43, 47), he was not expecting his followers to blind or maim themselves when tempted to sin. He was using a literary device known as hyperbole—extravagant exaggeration for effect—to make a lasting impression about dealing radically with the sin in our lives. He was making a serious point, even though he had no intention for people to take him literally. If Bible literalists did follow this verse literally, they would be an odd looking group!

It is essential to consider the literary form of a passage when determining its meaning. For instance, we cannot interpret poetic portions of the Bible in the same way in which we read the Law; and we can't read historical narrative in the same way in which we would personal letters. So, with those parts of the Bible that are clearly written in the style of apocalyptic literature, it is not right to ignore its highly symbolic nature. Likewise, we can't gloss over references to events that would have been easily understood by the original audience. Although claiming to champion the cause of literalism, premillennialists misuse some of the very texts they are eager to uphold.

Fulfillments: Then and Now

Inspired New Testament (NT) writers sometimes interpreted and explained OT prophecies in a way that would not have been obvious from the original context. For instance, Matthew 1:23 quotes Isaiah 7:14 to show that the virgin birth of Jesus "took place to fulfill what the Lord had said through the prophet" (Matthew 1:22). In Isaiah 7, however, the context is quite different. In its initial setting, God had instructed Isaiah to encourage the King of Judah with this news: his enemies, the kings of Aram and Samaria, would be dead inside the span of time necessary for a young woman to conceive, to bear a son and to teach him the difference between right and wrong. It is *only* because Matthew—an inspired writer—interprets the prophecy for us that we can possibly know that God was also referring to the birth of Jesus by Mary while she was still a virgin.

What does this have to do with premillennialism? Premillennialists claim to understand how events of today fulfill prophecies of long ago—with the confidence that can only come from divine inspiration. Even when the fulfillment of a prophecy can be shown to have already taken place historically, premillennialists insist that a "future fulfillment" is also meant. How is it possible to know this? Indeed, if the inspired NT writers had not interpreted certain passages of the Old Testament this way, we could not have made those identifications with any certainty. In some cases, we wouldn't have even known that a "prophecy" was being made! Who can claim to know that a particular prophecy, once fulfilled, is still awaiting "ultimate fulfillment" in a later context—without the benefit of inspiration? For example, who is to say that Russia is the "Army of the North" referred to in Scripture? Or that the beast with ten heads is the European Economic Community?

Israel Versus the Church

Premillennialism confuses the relationship between Israel and the church. According to dispensationalist writer Charles Ryrie, "The basic premise of Dispensationalism is two purposes of God expressed in the formation of two peoples who maintain their distinction throughout eternity."[1] Because dispensationalists approach Scripture with this premise in mind, a literal, earthly millennium and an elaborate end-time scenario become necessary. They think that if God made promises to Israel that have not been fulfilled for national, physical Israel, then there must be a future time when he plans to fulfill them—or else he is found to be a liar. For the premillennialist, these promises will be fulfilled during the time of the Tribulation and the Millennium.

This view of Scripture fails to account for several things. First, Abraham's descendents were not singled out to be favored for their own sake. Rather, God developed a nation in the land of Palestine through Abraham that would bless the world through the Messiah. As Loraine Boettner has observed, "But now that the Messiah has come and God's revelation to mankind has been completed, written in a book and made available to the people of all nations with nothing more to be added, there is no further need for a separate people or nation to serve that purpose."[2] Accordingly, "the dividing wall of hostility" between Jew and Gentile has been broken down (Ephesians 2:14-16), and it is now "those who are of faith who are sons of Abraham" (Galatians 3:7, NAS).

Second, NT writers apply to the church several key prophecies which were made to Israel. For example, Hosea 2:23 and 1:10 in Romans 9:24-26, or Jeremiah 31:31-34 in Hebrews 8:8-12. Jesus' disciples are now the inheritors of the promises made to God's people before the cross. Spiritually, we are now "the Israel of God" (Galatians 6:16).

Third, the New Covenant has nullified the first covenant. "By calling this covenant 'new,' he has made the first one obsolete; and what is obsolete and aging will soon disappear" (Hebrews 8:13). With the fall of Jerusalem and the destruction of the Temple in 70 AD by the armies of Rome, Biblical Judaism, along with its sacrificial system, came to an end. What is more, the supernatural rending of the curtain between the Holy Place and the Most Holy Place at the time of Jesus' death proclaimed that his final sacrifice had brought to an end the need for further sacrifice. The first covenant had served its purpose and was doomed to pass away, being displaced by the new covenant. The requirements of salvation today are no different for Jews than for Gentiles.

While nearly any view of Scripture finds it necessary to divide God's dealings with men into different "dispensations," the Darbyist dispensational system is fatally flawed. Its error lies in a failure to recognize that the Mosaic dispensation ended, thus it artificially prolongs the Jewish system to the end of the world. The idea that God has a future plan for Israel distinct from his plan for the rest of humanity is not consistent with the clear teaching of the Bible.

The Bride of Christ

His intent was that now, through the church, the manifold wisdom of God should be made known to the rulers and authorities in the heavenly realms, according to his eternal purpose which he accomplished in Christ Jesus our Lord. (Ephesians 3:10-11)

Premillennialists view the church as "a parenthesis" between the ministry of Jesus and his next coming. They see the church as an afterthought of Jesus when he "failed" to establish the kingdom among the Jews of his day. However, the Scriptures teach that the church is part of the eternal purpose of God. One reason for Jesus coming into the world was to establish his church

(Matthew 16:18-20). Jesus is spoken of as being the head of the church (Ephesians 1:22, 5:23; Colossians 1:18) and the foundation of the church (Ephesians 2:20).

Premillennialism does not show enough respect for the doctrine of the church. The church was both foreseen in prophecy and spoken of by the prophets. Here is what...

> ...the prophet Isaiah son of Amoz saw concerning Judah and Jerusalem:
>
> In the days to come
>   The mountain of the LORD's house
> Shall be established as the highest of the mountains,
>   And shall be raised above the hills;
> All the nations shall stream to it.
>   Many peoples shall come and say,
> "Come, let us go up to the mountain of the Lord,
>   to the house of the God of Jacob;
> that he may teach us his ways
>   and that we may walk in his paths."
> For out of Zion shall go forth instruction,
>   And the word of the LORD from Jerusalem. (Isaiah 2:1-4 NRSV)

The prophets of Israel had God's dreams placed on their hearts. Through inspiration, they saw things that others simply could not see. They saw what would truly be "a new world order," a new community and a deeper fellowship. Through God's power and the spirit of revelation, they broke free of a narrow nationalism and envisioned a worldwide family of believers united by a fresh, new relationship with God. Although we never hear the word "church" from the OT prophets, they clearly saw it coming and painted vivid pictures that would be fulfilled dramatically in the first century by Jesus, the apostles and the earliest disciples.

The Bible contains many specific prophecies about Christ and his beloved, the church, demonstrating that for generations God had the church on his heart and mind. He was waiting for the exact, perfect moment to unleash the glory of his spiritual kingdom in the world.

Before time began, God planned a way to draw humanity to him. Genesis 3:15 may be one of the first clues to his intention. He prophesied that the seed of woman would crush the head of the serpent, the first prophecy about the cross of Jesus. The seed that crushed Satan's head, Jesus, also became the foundation stone of the church.

Isaiah 2:1-4, quoted above, shows clearly that the coming "mountain of the Lord's house"—the church, the kingdom of God on earth (see Hebrews 12:18-23)—would be established in Jerusalem but be made up of all nations. The church would be an international fellowship, bridging racial extremes, social differences and economic boundaries. Even on the first day of its existence, as we read about it in the second chapter of Acts, we see the words of Isaiah being fulfilled. Men and women from all over the world streamed into the church and enjoyed a most uncommon fellowship. In Isaiah 11:6-9, the prophet again described the coming kingdom, saying it would bring natural enemies together. When Jesus came and led Jew and Gentile, slave and free, barbarian and Scythian into his church (Colossians 3:11), Isaiah's dream was fulfilled.

Joel 2:28-32 tells us of a great outpouring of the Spirit that would lead to people being saved—again, in Jerusalem. On the day of Pentecost, Peter called attention to God's miracles, which were evident for all to see, and he cited the fulfillment of this passage to begin his famed sermon that led to the conversion of the three thousand and the establishment of the church.

In Daniel 2:36-44, God gave a timetable for when the kingdom would come. A simple analysis of history reveals that the "fourth kingdom" (2:40) was the Roman Empire and "during the time of those kings" (2:44) refers to the Caesars of Rome. True to God's plan, this prophecy was fulfilled by the establishment of Jesus' church during the days of the Roman Empire which has now been in ruins for years—unlike God's everlasting kingdom, the church.

Before time began, God planned to build his church. It was not an afterthought. Like a careful architect, he drew up the plan detail by detail. He recorded these details for us to explore. We don't have to guess what the church should be like. And we don't have to wait for the millennium to see this plan realized. We can see the blueprints laid out across the pages of the Bible.

A number of years ago, I started a club based on the movie *Dead Poet's Society.* My club was called "The Dead Prophet's Society." On occasion, a few of my friends and I would gather to read our favorite scriptures to each other. We began each meeting by reading Luke 10:23-24:

Then he turned to his disciples and said privately, "Blessed are the eyes that see what you see. For I tell you that many prophets and kings wanted to see what you see but did not see it, and to hear what you hear but did not hear it."

Isn't it startling that we are able to see and hear things that the great kings and prophets of Israel longed to see and hear? King David would love to be in our places right now; Jeremiah would gladly trade places with us. Isaiah, Solomon, Micah, Hezekiah, Daniel, Josiah—we should marvel at the fact that they all would have loved to know what we know.

The church is not an afterthought of God. It is the fulfillment of hundreds of years of prophecy. It is one of God's greatest achievements. Be thankful that you can be a part of it today.

A Profusion of Confusion

Premill. Postmill. Amill. Obviously, not all of these views can be correct; some or all of them must necessarily be false. Why is there so much confusion and so many widely accepted ideas that are in conflict with much clear teaching of Scripture? Why are people so easily influenced to believe sensational end-time doctrines? And why should we even study eschatology when there are so many more practical matters to attend to? Why, oh why?

WHY FALSE DOCTRINE?

First, let's consider a number of reasons why false doctrine in general is so prevalent.

God Saw It Coming

The Bible predicted that false teaching would be widespread. God is not surprised by this development.

At that time many will turn away from the faith and will betray and hate each other, and many false prophets will appear and deceive many people. Because of the increase of wickedness, the love of most will grow cold.

Jesus, Matthew 24:10-12

I know that after I leave, savage wolves will come in among you and will not spare the flock. Even from your own number men will arise and distort the truth in order to draw away disciples after them.

Paul, Acts 20:29-30

The Spirit clearly says that in later times some will abandon the faith and follow deceiving spirits and things taught by demons. Such teachings come through hypocritical liars, whose consciences have been seared as with a hot iron. They forbid people to marry and order them to abstain from certain foods, which God created to be received with thanksgiving by those who believe and who know the truth.

Paul, 1 Timothy 4:1-3

As I study the Bible with someone to get them ready for baptism, I like to read passages like those found in 1 and 2 Timothy and Titus concerning Paul's attitude toward false doctrine. If we do not develop an understanding that false doctrine is sinful, wicked and destructive, then we will be "blown here and there by every wind of teaching" (Ephesians 4:14).

Jesus and Paul predicted that false teaching would be manifest and widespread. I often hear the question that if the Bible is true, why are there so many different churches and different doctrines

Examining Millennial Fever: The Year 2000 Crisis

The approach of the year 2000, which most regarded as the dawn of the new millennium, carried with it a sense of the unexpected. Doomsday prophets predicted the collapse of vital structures when January 1, 2000, rolled around because of the Y2K millennium computer bug. Books, magazines, Web sites and television shows were produced at a frantic pace to herald the many and various concerns of Y2K.

What do the magazine *Christianity Today* and the newspaper *The New York Times* have in common? For one thing, they both began 1999 by running articles highlighting evangelical Christianity's response to technology in the new millennium. In general, many evangelical Christians display a sense of fear of new technology, recently focused on the fear of the Y2K bug and its effect on our lives in the year 2000.

This focus on the Y2K bug is a small part of a bigger picture: the fear that many evangelical Christians have of new technology—including computers, medical advances in genetic studies, satellite- and video-monitoring systems, bar codes, cashless transactions and global politics. University of Wisconsin-Madison professor Paul Boyer described this fear in *Christianity Today* by saying,

"That the [end of time] tribulation could begin with a Y2K collapse...fits very closely into what the popularizers have been saying for years: the increasing reliance of society on technology and global electronic transfers of capital and information are paving the way for the antichrist's global control."[1] This type of fear mounted with the approach of the year 2000.

Grant R. Jeffrey's book, *Millennium Meltdown*, is a perfect illustration of Boyer's assessment. Jeffrey spent the first half of his book writing about the potential problems of the Y2K bug on our society. He quoted government authorities to demonstrate that the Y2K problem could have far-reaching consequences. His argument was persuasive. In chapter 11 of his book, he took a dramatic turn in his argument to say that the Y2K bug would be a tool the Antichrist would use to usher in a cashless world government. Jeffery writes:

"Those people dedicated to creating a New World Order realize that the only practical way to achieve their goal is to create an economic, political, or military crisis of such vast proportions that no nation, on its own, could possibly solve it. The Y2K computer crisis provides a unique opportunity to impose a global government solution."[2] Jeffery goes on to mention that the global elite had selected Mikhail Gorbachev to become one of the key leaders in the coming global government.

Some evangelical groups made preparations for a cataclysmic beginning (or end) in 2000 by preparing shelters stocked with food, water and medical supplies. Others withdrew their money from banks and placed their funds in shoe boxes hidden under floorboards in their homes.

The New York Times reported that the First Baptist Church of Doylestown, Pennsylvania, held a prayer meeting each week for people to ask God to intervene and to help find an answer to the Y2K bug. On the wall behind the altar of the church was projected the date of the prayer meeting. Underneath the date an ominous message appeared: "330 days left."

While no one knew exactly what would happen, the fact is that the Y2K bug hardly made a whimper when the year 2000 rolled around. The bigger problem was the hysteria that surrounded the potential problem. And not a few churches helped to propagate this hysteria.

Notes

1. Mark A. Kellner, "Y2K: A Secular Apocalypse?" *Christianity Today*, vol. 32, no. 1 (January 11, 1999) 60.

2. Grant R. Jeffery, *Millennium Meltdown: Spiritual and Practical Strategies to Survive Y2K* (Wheaton, Ill.: Tyndale House Pub., Inc., 1998) 153.

being taught in those churches? Actually, this argument speaks more for the truthfulness of the Bible than against it. The Biblical writers *predicted* that many would leave the true faith of the early church and turn to false doctrine. If we take a casual attitude toward false teaching, then our destiny may very well be the same as that of the false teachers. Is the Bible the standard for our belief and practice of Christianity? Do we know what the Bible teaches about eschatology? If not, we need to find out.

Searching for Hope

People are looking for something to believe in. Everyone is hungry for relationships and for meaning in their lives. They consult analysts before making simple decisions. They go to therapists who sit and listen—in other words, they pay big bucks to be heard by someone. One of the most amazing developments in modern society is the rise of "1-900" numbers which allow you to pay to have a conversation with someone, not to mention the hundreds and thousands of Internet chat rooms available any time of the day or night. For a few dollars or a dial-up access fee, you can talk to a complete stranger who will act as if he or she were your best friend and listen to you whine about whatever you wish to whine about. At one time, families and friends filled this void. These new trends in pop therapy demonstrate that people are hungry—they are looking for something.

In a town ten minutes from where I live in suburban U.S.A., there exists a community where witchcraft is openly advocated. These are not "evil" witches who ride brooms, turn children into frogs and have warts on their noses. This is a group of "white" witches whose main ambition is to live in harmony with nature and to tap into the goodness of Mother Earth. Recently, I noticed in a comic book store (yes, I frequent comic book stores and read comic books) a magazine published for teenage girls entitled *White Magic*. On the inside cover was an encouraging word to the parents that read, "Parents, this magazine promotes white witchcraft. This is a religion that has been practiced for centuries. It is a positive force in the lives of young people."

From movies like *Practical Magic*, starring Sandra Bullock and Nicole Kidman, to magazines for teenage girls—mysticism, new ageism, magic and the occult are chic and accepted. People are venturing into once unthinkable arenas in their search for meaning and hope.

Another evidence of this quest for hope is the sheer volume of self-help books that are being generated today. If you go into your local bookstore and browse through the self-help section, you will be amazed. Books that promote weight loss, greater self-esteem, "spirituality" or health and nutrition are being produced in rapid succession. Why is so much being written on this topic? Because people will buy it. People are hungry to make their lives better. They want hope.

Hope can come in the here and now, or it can come in the hereafter. Books on end-time prophecy offer hope in the hereafter. But if the hope is built on teaching that is un-Biblical, it is offering no hope at all. We must know what the Bible says about end-time issues so that we can offer people real hope.

'Itching Ears'

In the presence of God and of Christ Jesus, who will judge the living and the dead, and in view of his appearing and his kingdom, I give you this charge: Preach the Word; be prepared in season and out of season; correct, rebuke and encourage—with great patience and careful instruction. For the time will come when men will not put up with sound doctrine. Instead, to suit their own desires, they will gather around them a great number of teachers

to say what their itching ears want to hear. They will turn
their ears away from the truth and turn aside to myths.
Paul, 2 Timothy 4:1-4

People have itching ears for what is easy, dramatic or
mysterious. For example, ask yourself the following questions: If
you had the choice of losing weight by (1) swallowing a pill and
then eating anything you wanted to eat, or by (2) exercising every
day and eating only one-fourth of what you eat now, which
would you choose? If you could select between a job that
stimulates your intellect, imagination and energy, and one which
is laborious and uninspiring, which would you select?

We desire things that excite us, which is why big, blockbuster
summer action films like *Star Wars* always do better at the box
office than highbrow, artsy films like *Sense and Sensibility*.
People want to be entertained.

The latest books and videos on premillennial doctrine are
certainly dramatic and entertaining. It is fascinating to think about
what the seven years after the Rapture might be like. What will
happen to those who are left behind? Tim LaHaye and Jerry
Jenkins have sold millions of books in their *Left Behind* series,
dramatically portraying what life will be like during this time. As
previously noted, their books have become the biggest selling
"Christian" novel series in history.

Premillennial doctrine sells books, but is it Biblical? Doctrine
should not be based on what our "itching ears" want to hear, but
on what the Holy Spirit revealed to the apostles. We must know
the difference.

Greedy for Gain

But there were also false prophets among the people, just as there will be false teachers among you. They will secretly introduce destructive heresies, even denying the sovereign Lord who bought them—bringing swift destruction on themselves. Many will follow their shameful ways and will bring the way of truth into disrepute. In their greed these teachers will exploit you with stories they have made up. Their condemnation has long been hanging over them, and their destruction has not been sleeping.

Peter, 2 Peter 2:1-3

If anyone teaches false doctrines and does not agree to the sound instruction of our Lord Jesus Christ and to godly teaching, he is conceited and understands nothing. He has an unhealthy interest in controversies and quarrels about words that result in envy, strife, malicious talk, evil suspicions and constant friction between men of corrupt mind, who have been robbed of the truth and who think that godliness is a means to financial gain.

Paul, 1 Timothy 6:3-5

Religion is big business. George Orwell, author of *Animal Farm* and *1984*, wrote to a friend in 1938 that "there might be a lot of cash in starting a new religion." Yes, there is money to be made in religion. But to make the money, you have to give the people what they want.

Since the Holy Spirit established sound doctrine in the early church, false doctrine has always been there as an alternative. Often, false doctrine offers an easier, cheaper grace. False doctrine sometimes sounds better, is more tolerant and is easier to digest. And preachers are ready to preach it. It can fill the pews, build nice buildings, be broadcast by satellite across the world. Religion sells. Especially when it caters to people's laziness, sinfulness, materialism and naivete. Why is false doctrine so prevalent today? People will buy it.

The Fear Factor

For centuries religious leaders have used fear to motivate people to get right with God. Yes, the Bible does teach that we must fear the Lord, but this is meant more as a healthy respect for God. Yes, the Bible gives us pictures of hell as a deterrent to choosing evil. But the overwhelming emphasis of Scripture is to follow God because it's right, good, grace-filled and wise.

I want my children to respect me to the point that when I ask them to do something, they are responsive. But I do not want my children to be afraid of me. When the disciples of Jesus were afraid, Jesus tried to dispel their fears. He wants our respect, not our fear.

Certain views of the millennium can play on people's fears. Here are a few: fear of being left behind when the Rapture comes; fear of the Antichrist and the mark of the beast; fear of the great, final battle of Armageddon; fear of having to suffer through the intense persecution pictured in the final three-and-a-half years of the seven-year tribulation. Fears abound in premillennial doctrine. However, doctrine should motivate us to draw closer to God because of his grace, not to be scared closer to God because of our fears.

Looking at the last two points, you may wonder how religion can give people what they want and, at the same time, play on their fears. It may seem as though these are contradictory. The answer may lie in the fact that most premillennial theology gives people sensational views of the end, but then offers an easy believism as the solution. People are frightened into a response that ends up calling for very little from them personally.

WHY WE NEED KNOWLEDGE

Now we will turn to answering the question of why we need to know about false doctrine.

Always Prepared

But in your hearts set apart Christ as Lord. Always be prepared to give an answer to everyone who asks you to give the reason for the hope that you have. But do this with gentleness and respect, keeping a clear conscience, so that those who speak maliciously against your good behavior in Christ may be ashamed of their slander.

Peter, 1 Peter 3:15-16

We must be ready to answer people's questions. For example, if you met a Jehovah's Witness on the street and he or she began to teach that God was going to establish a millennial kingdom that would last a thousand years on the earth, would you be able to explain to them that the kingdom has already come upon the earth in the form of the church? If a Universalist were to teach you that at the end God was going to save everything and everyone, could you show them their error? If a Catholic were to try to impress upon you the legitimacy of purgatory, could you demonstrate the fallacy of this teaching? We must develop a love for the truth so that we can steer clear of falsehood and help others who have misunderstood or been misled.

Life to the Full

The truth of the Second Coming of Jesus is an important doctrine. What we believe about this affects the way we live life in the here and now. We must be able to answer people's questions concerning this doctrine, especially at the dawn of a new millennium. So much has been said about the Second Coming that confusion abounds. This can be a launching point to begin spiritual conversations with many people. If we look like we don't know what we are talking about when this topic is brought up, then it might prevent someone from wanting to talk to us about other spiritual topics. This does not mean that we need to be a walking Bible encyclopedia (although a few of those in our churches wouldn't be a bad idea!), but we must be informed. Are you informed on what the Bible teaches about the end of time?

> There are many reasons why the modern Christian and even the modern theologian may hesitate to give to the doctrine of Christ's Second Coming that emphasis which was usually laid on it by our ancestors. Yet it seems to me impossible to retain in any recognizable form our belief in the Divinity of Christ and the truth of the Christian revelation while abandoning, or even persistently neglecting, the promised, and threatened, Return.[1]
>
> *C. S. Lewis, literary critic and writer*

Doctrine and Salvation

Watch your life and doctrine closely. Persevere in them, because if you do, you will save both yourself and your hearers.

Paul, 1 Timothy 4:16

I'm sure you've heard, as I often have, that doctrine is not all that important. Growing up in the Bible Belt (in the southern US), people would say, "It is not important what you believe, just as long as you believe in God and in Jesus." In other words, doctrine doesn't matter; only faith matters. The apostle Paul would take exception to this. Paul taught that we must watch both our life and our doctrine closely. Both are a matter of salvation. Although the teaching about how Jesus will come to judge the world doesn't seem as important as getting someone off of drugs or keeping someone faithful in his or her marriage, how we understand the doctrine of the end of time is important and can become a matter of salvation.

Having said this, I want to be clear that we will not be judged on how well we understand the doctrine of the end-time. Attempts to understand various aspects of end-time prophecy and apocalyptic writing have led great minds to differing conclusions for nearly two thousand years. In fact, an exact knowledge of the events surrounding the end of time will not be possible until they have taken place![2] No, our understanding of the millennium per se will not determine our eternity. However, a misunderstanding or a misguided emphasis on these doctrines has led to some tragic practices in the history of Christianity. Beyond this, an acceptance of sloppy methods of interpretation in this particular area can lead to the same thing in areas that do directly affect salvation.

Our doctrine of the end of time can affect the way we live today. For instance, if we believe that Jesus is coming like a thief,[3] then we must be ready at all times for his return. Or if we believe in purgatory, then we assume that people will have a second chance after death—which takes away a motivation for evangelism, as well as an urgency to get right with God here and now. How we view the future affects the way we live in the present. This is why eschatology is important. By paying careful attention to God's word, we can dispel the clouds of confusion that often surround this issue. Having done so, we can get on with living lives that are worthy of the great King who is coming again in glory.

The Late Great Planet Earth

Face red, veins
Protruding
As he yells and yelps
And rants and raves
About a day soon
Soon a day
When the Lord
Will come
And bring peace with a sword
A sword of peace
On the Late Great Planet Earth.

Wars and rumors
Of wars
Armies preparing
For battle
On the plain of Megiddo
Armageddon Time
As they drink the wine
Of vengeance for
The saints
Marching, marching
The Saints go marching against
The Army of Darkness
On the Late Great Planet Earth.

Faceless dictator
With a beastly mark
Unites a cashless people
In a New World Order
To rebuild the temple
Where appears
Abomination
That persecutes God's people
In a beastly way
On the Late Great Planet Earth.

The sign of the time
Here and Now
Here and There
And Everywhere
People get ready
To take flight and
Meet the Lord in
The air
And leave the rest
The Remnant remains
To fight the beast
In beastly fashion
On the Late Great Planet Earth.

Good Drama
Remnants and
Battles
Make for good novels
But that's not
The plan
That's not the way
The Good Books says
Says the Good Book
How it will be
Trumpet will sound
Dead will rise
The earth will melt
Melt with a great fire and
Thus will end time
Time will end
On the Late Great Planet Earth.

–G. Steve Kinnard

The Bible Tells Me So

3

Old Testament Verses

As Christians, our standard for faith and practice is the inspired Word of God—the Bible (2 Timothy 3:16-17). Therefore we need to approach our study of the end of time (or any other subject, for that matter!) by a careful examination of relevant passages of Scripture. By removing verses from their historical and textual settings, it is possible for end-time soothsayers to paint any number of elaborate views of the end of the world. However, we must not shy away from passages that have been used to support a particular position. Instead, we need to draw conclusions that are in agreement with "the whole will of God" (Acts 20:27) by considering these verses in context.

As surprising as it may sound to some, there are no OT passages that explicitly teach the concept of a millennium. The following Scriptures contain verses that have been understood by some as describing elements of a millennial scenario. Yet, interpreting these passages in context leads to a different conclusion.

ISAIAH

Isaiah began his prophetic work in the year Uzziah died, approximately 740 BC, and he was still active with Hezekiah during the siege of Jerusalem by Sennacherib in 701 BC. Writing from Judah, he prophesied about the Assyrian captivity of the northern kingdom and wrote about Judah and the surrounding nations as well.

Chapter 11

The book of Isaiah contains some of the most amazing messianic prophecies found in Scripture. Chapter 11 clearly prophesies about Jesus, the descendant of Jesse, who will come with the Spirit and power of the Lord. Verses 6-9 describe the nature of his church—not some future millennial kingdom when all the animals will live in harmony with one another. Natural enemies are described as being at peace with each other, oppressors and oppressed—getting along. This is a description of the loving, inclusive nature of the church in which each and every person is accepted as a brother or sister in Christ (Galatians 3:28, Colossians 3:11).

EZEKIEL

The prophet Ezekiel received his call in 592 BC, the fifth year after Jehoiakim was captured. He prophesied through the twenty-seventh year (571 BC) of the exile in Babylon; thus, his ministry spanned some twenty years.

The notable and influential families of Jerusalem were carried into Babylon in 597 BC and Ezekiel was taken with this wave of exiles. He prophesied to convince the exiles that Jerusalem and the temple were going to fall because of God's righteous judgment upon the people of Israel. But Israel was not to despair, for from the ruins, God would rebuild his city and reestablish the kingdom of Israel. This took place in part when the Jews were allowed to return to Jerusalem some seventy years later under men like Zerubbabel, Ezra and Nehemiah. It reached its ultimate fulfillment in the establishment of Jesus' church.

Chapters 36–37

Chapter 36:1-15. God promised the exiles hope as he declared that the mountains of Israel would be restored to their original splendor. The restoration would occur in the cities as well.

Chapter 36:16-38. An outstanding theological section of Ezekiel is found here in chapter 36. Ezekiel spoke of God restoring fortune to Israel because of his own name's sake— because other nations were not respecting him after Israel's destruction. God would take the initiative to rebuild Israel, giving them a new heart, a new spirit and a new covenant. All these were symbols of the church. (See Hebrews 8:8-12.)

Chapter 37:1-14. Ezekiel was taken in a vision to a valley filled with dry bones. He was told to prophesy in order for the bones to come to life and be filled with breath. He did and a vast army stood before him. Those in exile felt like dry bones, yet God had the power to recreate and restore life. The "resurrection" pictured here was a resurrection of their cause, a vindication of the exiled people of Israel.

Chapter 37:15-28. Ezekiel took two sticks (one for Israel and one for Judah) and made one stick. In the same way God would unite all of Israel once again in one kingdom. This message signals the arrival of the church, God's future kingdom, that would include all humanity.

Chapters 38–39

Ezekiel 38-39 contain prophecies about God. These prophecies are apocalyptic in nature and could be subversive writings of Ezekiel *against* Babylon. The purpose was to show that God was the Lord of history and that he would accomplish everything according to his will. These chapters are referred to in apocalyptic fashion in the New Testament (Revelation 20:8).

Chapter 38:1-10. Introduction of the prophecies concerning God.

Chapter 38:11-23. God defended a defenseless Israel in a cosmic battle where righteousness would win over evil. In graphic terms, the imminent defeat of Israel's enemies is being described.

Chapter 39:1-29 Gog would be so devastated that Israel would use its spears as firewood for seven years and would bury its dead for seven months. This describes a total defeat and destruction of the forces of evil in this cosmic battle.

DANIEL

Like Ezekiel, Daniel was a prophet of the exile in Babylon. His prophecies can be dated around 536 BC. Daniel served the courts of Nebuchadnezzar, Belshazzar, Darius the Mede and Cyrus.

The book of Daniel effectively shows the providence of God in the world as he deals with his people who are among the "Gentiles." God raises a world power to strength and destroys it because of its rebellion. At the same time God is loyal to his covenant people.

Chapter 2

Nebuchadnezzar has a dream that he cannot remember. Nebuchadnezzar asks all the sages and religious leaders in his kingdom to tell him his dream. They all fail. Finally, Daniel tells the dream and its meaning to the king.

The dream concerns an image that is made of four parts. Each section represents a kingdom. The head of gold is the glorious Babylonian kingdom of which Nebuchadnezzar is king. The chest and arms of silver represented the next kingdom on the scene: the Medo-Persian Empire. Following the Medo-Persian kingdom was the impressive Greek Empire of Alexander the Great represented by a belly and thighs of bronze. After this kingdom would come the great Roman Empire represented by legs of iron and feet of iron and clay. During this last empire (the Roman Empire), a kingdom would come that was to be greater than any of the others. Because it is an eternal kingdom, it is the one Jesus would build in the New Testament. The prophecy does not speak about the end of time, but rather, it directs God's chosen people to pay attention to when God's promised Messiah would build his kingdom: during the Roman Empire.

Chapters 7–12

Daniel has a dream about four beasts which come up out of the sea. After these beasts, the Ancient of Days announces the coming of a universal and everlasting Messiah.

Chapter 8. Two years after the previous vision, Daniel has a vision of a ram and a he-goat. The he-goat defeats the ram. This vision represents the toppling of the Medo-Persian kingdom by the Greeks, which occurred in 330 BC. Later, Greece would be divided into smaller kingdoms, and all of this would happen before God's kingdom came into the world.

Chapter 9. Daniel confesses the sins of his people and himself before God, asking favor upon Jerusalem. Gabriel gave Daniel a vision concerning God's judgment upon Jerusalem and its ultimate desolation, which occurred in 70 AD.

Chapter 10. Daniel saw a vision of a great war. After fighting a battle in the heavens, Gabriel delivers a message to Daniel in a vision.

Chapters 11 and 12. Daniel received a glimpse of the future of Israel. The Jews would be persecuted and oppressed, especially during the reign of Antiochus Epiphanes (175-164 BC). The nation would eventually be delivered and those who had stood firm and stayed faithful would be blessed.

ZECHARIAH

The messages recorded in the first half of the book of Zechariah were most likely given between 519-518 BC. The messages recorded in the last half of the book probably come from a somewhat later period in Zechariah's life, and most conservative scholars would date chapters 9-14 between 480 and 470 BC.

Chapters 1–8

By means of eight visions (1:7-6:8), God shows postexilic Israel that Jerusalem and the temple would be rebuilt, the priesthood cleansed, and peace and safety restored to the land. "The Branch," Jesus, is promised to Israel (6:9-15), and prosperity is deemed inevitable when the presence of the Lord returns to Zion (8:1-23).

Chapters 9–14

Zechariah 9-14 offers a message of hope to Israel. After Zechariah witnessed the rebuilding of the temple in 516 BC, he turned his gaze to the future of Israel. God showed Zechariah that a new day was dawning for Israel in which the quality of life for God's people would improve. The presence of God's Spirit in the community would add a new dynamic to their lives. In the new Messianic community, a Davidic king would rule over the people, and a Levitical priest would sit at his side (6:9-14). The new age would not be just for the Jews to enjoy, but the Gentiles would be offered an opportunity to participate in this new community (8:20-23). All would be offered a place in this community because God would be crowned "king over all the earth" in that day (14:9). This would be a world community where justice, peace, truth and plenty would reside in the land (8:4-5). During this time, Yahweh would demonstrate his sovereign rule by punishing all the enemies of Israel and exalting his people above all people. These passages all find their fulfillment in the church that Jesus established.

It makes sense that the great prophets of the Old Testament were more interested in the *first coming* of the Messiah whom they had never met, than they were in his return. The kingdom they longed for did not fail to come, as premillennialists claim.[1]

> Concerning this salvation, the prophets, who spoke of the grace that was to come to you, searched intently and with the greatest care, trying to find out the time and circumstances to which the Spirit of Christ in them was pointing when he predicted the sufferings of Christ and the glories that would follow. It was revealed to them that they were not serving themselves but you, when they spoke of the things that have now been told you by those who have preached the gospel to you by the Holy Spirit sent from heaven. Even angels long to look into these things. (1 Peter 1:10-12)

We should be in awe of the way God inspired his prophets to speak about what we now experience in the church! We will now turn our attention to the New Testament to see if we find any support for the doctrine of premillennialism there.

New Testament Verses

In this chapter, we will look at NT passages of Scripture that are relevant to our discussion of end-time prophecy. Once again, an understanding of context will prove invaluable for interpreting these texts.

Mark 13:1–37: The Little Apocalypse

Evidence shows that John Mark wrote his Gospel before the other three wrote theirs. In doing so, he invented a new literary genre, the theological biography. Matthew and Luke then based their Gospels on Mark's. This being the case, we will investigate the apocalyptic sections of the Gospel of Mark first.

As Jesus left the Temple Mount with his disciples to travel over to the Mount of Olives and back to Bethany to spend the night, the disciples comment about the beauty of the temple, making special mention of its massive stones. King Herod's builders had freshly cut these stones as he had the temple reconstructed and extended the borders of the Temple Mount to the north, south and west. Some of these impressive stones are visible today, weighing as much as a 747 airliner. It was a tremendous feat of engineering to build the temple complex.

In order to correctly interpret this passage, we need to pay close attention to the question Jesus was answering as he began to speak. Jesus commented that not one stone of the temple would be left on another—in other words, the temple was going to be destroyed. The disciples wanted to know when this would happen. The events described in the rest of the chapter answer this question.

Before the temple was to be destroyed, what would occur? The following signs are mentioned: false messiahs, wars and rumors of wars, earthquakes, famines, persecution of the church, the gospel preached to all nations, the abomination of desolation, sun and moon darkened, stars will fall from the sky, heavenly bodies will shake, the Son of Man will come in the clouds and angels are sent to gather the elect.

Some of these signs seem to signify that Jesus is speaking of his Second Coming and the end of time. But note that throughout the entire discourse, he is answering the one question posed by the disciples of when the temple will be destroyed. Two of Jesus' comments placed the answer to that question in the near future— during the apostles' lifetime.

First, in verse 14 Jesus tells the disciples to pay close attention to the signs and flee from Jerusalem when they occur, which places the events in the lifetime of the apostles. We know from early church history that the disciples did trust the promise of Jesus, and when they saw the signs, they fled "to the hills" over the Jordan River to places like Pella and began Christian communities there. Those who did not understand the signs of Jesus suffered through the bloodbath that resulted when the Tenth Roman Legion wreaked havoc on Jerusalem and destroyed the temple.

Second, in verse 30 Jesus specifically promises that the events described would be fulfilled in the apostles' ("this") generation. "All these events" were to happen while they were living. This means that even the events that seem to describe the Second Coming of Jesus had to occur before the destruction of the temple in 70 AD.

The Son of Man came in the clouds and the angels gathered the elect. The sun and moon were darkened. This is where an appreciation for literary genre becomes invaluable, for all of these expressions are typical of apocalyptic language. It is heavily symbolic. In fact, the OT prophets often described the downfall of a nation in these graphic terms (e.g. Isaiah 13:10—judgment on Babylon; Nahum 1:3-6—judgment on Ninevah). Did Jesus actually come in the clouds before the destruction of the temple? Possibly he did, but more likely this is language of judgment found throughout the Old Testament. The destruction of the temple in Jerusalem was God's judgment on the Jewish nation. Jesus coming in the clouds is a symbol to say that the judgment of heaven had come upon Israel.

Is it wrong to take the signs and events given by Jesus in Mark 13 and place them in a calendar of pre-Rapture or pre-Tribulation events? In a word, yes. All the events of Mark 13 have already transpired. They happened just before or when the Roman army sacked Jerusalem and destroyed the temple of God in 70 AD. Even the warning to "watch" and "be alert" applied to the disciples of the first century. The disciples did "watch" and they were "alert"; therefore they escaped the destruction of the temple and fled across the Jordan to safety.

So, what can we learn from Mark 13? We should learn to trust the promises of God. The verse that speaks loudest to me is verse 31, "Heaven and earth will pass away, but my words will never pass away." Jesus promised that the temple would be destroyed when the events described transpired, and it happened just like he said it would happen. Today we must trust all the promises of Jesus in our lives.

Matthew 24:1–51: The Long Apocalypse

In Matthew 24, Matthew gives a longer, fuller description of Jesus' teaching concerning the destruction of the temple. In verse three the disciples ask Jesus two questions: First, they want to know when the temple will be destroyed. Second, they want to know the signs associated with his coming and the end of the age. The key in this passage is to understand exactly when he began answering each question.

In verses 4-35, Jesus describes the events surrounding the destruction of the temple. In verse 36 he makes a transition to his

Second Coming and the end of the age. Notice how closely verses 4-35 tie into the description given by Mark concerning the temple's destruction. Jesus mentions the following signs: false messiahs, wars and rumors of wars, famines, earthquakes, persecution, increase of wickedness, the gospel preached to the whole world as a testimony to all nations, the abomination of desolation, the sun and moon darkened, stars fall and planets shake, the Son of Man comes in the clouds and angels gather the elect.

Once again, some of these signs seem to speak about the Second Coming of Jesus, namely, the gospel preached to the whole world, Jesus coming in the clouds, and the angels gathering the elect. But again, two sayings place these events in the context of the first century. First, the disciples are told to flee to the mountains of Judea when they see these signs (verse 16). These signs were given to the early Christians as a warning to get out of Jerusalem, saving themselves from the coming massacre by the Roman army. Second, "all these things" were to happen in their "generation," not ours.

In verse 36, Jesus makes a transition to answering the second question posed by the disciples. When would he come, and when would time end? Verse 37 states that Jesus is now describing how it will be "at the coming of the Son of Man." First, it will be sudden, unexpected, no signs given and like a thief. Thus, there is no need to try to predict the Second Coming of Jesus. The angels know nothing of that time, so there is no need to ask them. The Son doesn't even know anything about that time, so he can't tell you— only the Father knows. This is very different from the obvious signs that would precede the destruction of the temple. Now Jesus speaks of absolute secrecy—no signs, no clues. Since only the Father knows, who are we to presume to predict this date? What arrogance on the part of any minister to claim to know what the angels and the Son do not know!

Second, this event is described in terms of the resurrection as described in 1 Thessalonians 4. "One will be taken and the other left" describes how those who are alive when Jesus comes will be caught up in the clouds with Jesus. This is not the Rapture described by the premillennialists, but it is part of the resurrection process. Everyone—good or bad—who is alive at that time will be taken to judgment. They will experience the pleasure of the master (v46) or the weeping and gnashing of teeth (v51).

What do we learn here? When Jesus comes to judge the world, it will be without warning, with no signs or omens. He will come like a thief, therefore there is no need to attempt to predict when this will happen. In fact, it is simply arrogant to do so. We must be ready at all times—we must always be prepared to meet Jesus.

Matthew 25:1–46: The End of Time

Jesus continues his discourse concerning the end of time into chapter 25 of Matthew. Remember, the early copies of the Scriptures had no chapter divisions; there would have been no break between chapters 24 and 25.

Jesus tells two parables that each have something to say about the end of time. The Parable of the Ten Virgins (25:1-13) is a reminder to always be watching for the return of the Messiah. He will return unannounced to surprise those who are not ready for his coming.

The Parable of the Talents (25:14-30) reminds us that we will be judged according to how we have used the gifts that God has given us. Have we made good use of our gifts, or have we used them selfishly? The Messiah will have something to say about how we have used our talents when he returns.

Jesus then gives us his greatest portrayal of what the final judgment scene will entail in verses 31-46. Here Jesus (the Son of Man) sits upon a throne of judgment before all of humanity. He divides everyone into two groups—the sheep and the goats. People are divided based upon how they treated others while they were living. Jesus then says,

> "I was hungry and you gave me something to eat; I was thirsty and you gave me something to drink; I was a stranger and you invited me in; I needed clothes and you clothed me; I was sick and you looked after me; and I was in prison and you came to visit me" (vv35-36).

The goats will go away to eternal punishment and the righteous to eternal life. This is the scene of final judgment. There is no hint of a second chance or purgatory here and certainly no mention of failing to make the Rapture and then getting a second chance. You live your life, you die and then you face judgment.

Luke 21:5–38: The Apocalypse of Luke

The apocalypse of Luke is shaped around the apocalypses of Mark (Mark 13) and Matthew (Matthew 24). Jesus answers the question raised in verse seven concerning the time of the destruction of the temple. All the signs given here refer to the destruction of the Jewish temple in 70 AD. Because he is writing to Gentiles, some of the veiled references that would have been more familiar to Matthew's readers have been interpreted for a non-Jewish audience. Instead of

> "So when you see standing in the holy place 'the abomination that causes desolation,' spoken of through the prophet Daniel—let the reader understand—then let those who are in Judea flee to the mountains." (Matthew 24:15-16)

Luke writes,

> "When you see Jerusalem being surrounded by armies, you will know that its desolation is near. Then let those who are in Judea flee to the mountains, let those in the city get out, and let those in the country not enter the city. For this is the time of punishment in fulfillment of all that has been written." (Luke 21:20-22)

The "abomination of desolation" refers to the desecration of the temple in 70 AD. Those who had listened to Jesus' words would know it was time to flee Jerusalem in advance of the approaching Romans and head for the hills along the Jordan.

It is wrong to take these signs and place them in a doctrine of the end of time. Even the sign that the Son of Man would come in a cloud with power and great glory refers to the destruction of the temple. This was a coming *in judgment* upon Israel.

It is not just bad exegesis, but it is simply wrong to take this passage and propose that the temple of God must be rebuilt in Jerusalem before Jesus returns. Evangelical Christians have been pumping millions of dollars into Israel, believing this would speed the coming of Jesus. These same people often turn a deaf ear to the plight of thousands of suffering, poor, persecuted Arab Christians who believe in Jesus. This is wrong—sinfully wrong.

Luke 21:32 says plainly, "I tell you the truth, this generation will certainly not pass away until all these things have happened. Heaven and earth will pass away, but my words will never pass away." Jesus lets us know with certainty that these signs were given to the disciples of the first century, "this generation." He bet his word on it. Let us take him at his word and apply these signs to the events surrounding the destruction of the temple of Jerusalem in 70 AD.

John 5:28–29: Jesus and the Resurrection

Do not be amazed at this, for a time is coming when all who are in their graves will hear his voice and come out—those who have done good will rise to live, and those who have done evil will rise to be condemned. (John 5:28-29)

A central tenant of premillennialism is the belief that two resurrections will occur, and they will take place one thousand years apart. The teachings of Jesus contradict this. Jesus speaks of "a time"—also translated "the hour"—when the righteous and the unrighteous will be raised. Paul echoes this when he tells Felix, the Roman governor, that "there will be a resurrection of both the righteous and the wicked" (Acts 24:15). Don't look for two resurrections; there will only be one.

Romans 8:17–23: Redemption of Creation

In this fascinating passage of Scripture, Romans 8:17-23, Paul speaks of creation groaning for redemption in the same way that the human body longs for a new, spiritual body. Paul uses the literary technique of personification to give to the earth human qualities of thinking, feeling and expression. This verse teaches that when Jesus comes, he will redeem creation. Creation has had to suffer the effects of sin just like humanity. The redemption of creation will not come one thousand years after Jesus comes, as premillennialism teaches. It will come when Jesus comes.

How will this occur? Only God knows. According to 1 Peter 3:3-14 this earth will be destroyed with intense heat. A new heaven and a new earth will be formed. Will the earth die and experience resurrection like humanity? These are mysteries that only God can answer.

Romans 11: One Salvation for All

Premillennialists love Romans 11. Denominational Jewish Christians love this scripture as well. This passage is used as a pretext to support the agenda of the modern nation of Israel. The passage shows that Paul used his ministry to the Gentiles to attract the Jews. According to premillennialism, when a full number of Gentiles are reached, then God will save "all" the Jews. As a result, they claim that Christians must support Israel, because it is a part of God's remnant.

I have spoken with evangelical Christians living in Israel who believe that there is no reason to evangelize Jews. They believe that "all Israel" will be saved in the end, so why is there a need to preach to them about Jesus? They believe that at the resurrection every Jew will be made to realize that Jesus is the Messiah and be saved. Is this what Paul had in mind in Romans 11?

If we took this verse out of context, it might say this. But we must remember how Paul redefined Judaism in chapter two. Romans 2:25-27 says that circumcision has no value if you break the law. Continuing, he insists that

"A man is not a Jew if he is only one outwardly, nor is circumcision merely outward and physical. No, a man is a Jew if he is one inwardly; and circumcision is circumcision of the heart, by the Spirit, not by the written code." (Romans 2:28-29)

This Israel, this Jew, this circumcised believer, as defined by Paul, will be a part of the "all Israel" that will be saved.

For not all who are descended from Israel are Israel. Nor because they are his descendants are they all Abraham's children. (Romans 9:6-7)

God no longer has a chosen nation physically. But anyone who repents and is baptized in the name of Jesus—is inwardly circumcised—can be a part of his spiritual nation.

If Paul believed that "all Israel" were to be saved without Jesus, then why did he risk his life to preach to the Jews? Even as an apostle to the Gentiles, he still entered the Jewish synagogues to preach to his Jewish brothers about the necessity of embracing Jesus as Lord. Everyone needs to accept Jesus as Lord to be saved (John 14:6, Acts 4:12). They must accept him in the here and now. To wait until the end of time is to wait until it is too late.

1 Corinthians 15:12–28: The Church

One of the central teachings on the resurrection is found in 1 Corinthians 15. Premillennialism teaches the necessity of two resurrections: one during the Rapture and one after the Tribulation. However, in this chapter (Paul's longest teaching on the subject of the resurrection), we see only one resurrection, which comes at the end of time.

First, Paul says that Jesus will reign until he puts all his enemies under his feet, and the last enemy to be destroyed will be death. Premillennialists take this to describe the millennial kingdom of Jesus on the earth. Jesus will reign on the earth and then fight the final battle of Armageddon in which he will destroy every enemy—even death.

But Paul mentions in the next verse that Jesus has already put everything under his feet. On the cross, Jesus won the greatest victory. Everything is already under the power of Jesus. In him we are "more than conquerors." This does not describe some future millennial kingdom. It is descriptive of the church which we can be a part of today. Today we can be a part of God's eternal kingdom. We should take great delight in this.

Philippians 3:20–21: A New Body

Paul, in Philippians 3:20-21, teaches about the transformation of our bodies at the resurrection. We will be changed from a "lowly" body into a "glorious" body. The mortal will put on immortality; the physical will become spiritual. When Jesus comes, we will be changed into a more glorious body—a more spiritual body.

1 Thessalonians 4:13–5:11: Rapture Vs. Judgment

The premillennialists set up camp and have a revival in chapters four and five of 1 Thessalonians. This is where the concept of the Rapture is found. The saved will be raptured or caught up in the air to meet Christ. But notice the word "rapture" does not appear here—or anywhere else in the Bible. It is an anglicized form of the Latin word *rapiemur,* meaning "caught up." What is Paul teaching here?

First of all, the popular idea of a "secret" rapture (first proposed in the nineteenth century) finds no support here. The "loud command," the "voice of the archangel" and "the trumpet call of God" that accompany the coming of the Lord would make it the noisiest "secret" ever told! Jesus' return will be anything but secret.

In context, Paul is comforting the early church concerning disciples who have already died: they are waiting for the return of

Jesus. When Jesus returns for the last judgment, the dead will rise first. Then the rest—those who are still alive at the time of his return—will rise to meet Jesus in the air. This is the scene of the final return of Jesus. The world will end. No one will be left behind.

To take this verse and build a doctrine of the Rapture of the church is wrong. The church will not be caught up, but *every living person* will be caught up to face judgment. This is the description of the last days as given by Paul.

The next section (5:1-11) makes it clear that Paul is speaking of the Second Coming of Jesus. He describes the coming like a thief—unannounced—with surprise. The point is this: Always be ready. Don't trust in signs; trust in God and be ready each and every moment to meet Jesus. Constant vigilance is the key.

2 Thessalonians 1:5–2:12: The Man of Lawlessness

A time when Christ will come to judge both the righteous and the wicked is the topic of 2 Thessalonians 1:5-2:12. This will occur when Jesus is revealed from heaven in blazing fire with his powerful angels. This passage depicts a final judgment scene in which Jesus will come as a thief in the night to end time and begin eternity.

Paul's first letter to the church in Thessalonica did not address all of their questions about the Second Coming. In this second letter, he hopes to clear up the confusion. He mentions here a "man of lawlessness." Premillennialists take this to be a personal Antichrist who has the mark of the beast. Taking a pinch of 2 Thessalonians, a dash of 1 John, and a touch of Revelation, they conjure up a powerful figure who will precede the great Tribulation of the church: the Antichrist. When you look at each passage on its own, you begin to see that the Bible does not speak of a powerful, end-time political and religious leader known as the Antichrist. This is the creation of preachers with very active imaginations.

Let's see who this "man of lawlessness" is in this passage. Here, Paul is trying to correct confusion regarding the coming of Jesus. Some have said that Jesus had already come—but he had not. Before Jesus comes, the "man of lawlessness" must come. He will exalt himself over God to be worshiped as a god. He will set himself up in God's temple. This description is reminiscent of what were surely some of the most humiliating and appalling episodes in Jewish history: the desecration of their temple. The most infamous example was when the Seleucid king Antiochus Epiphanes offered a pig on the altar and carried off temple treasuries in 168 BC, prompting the Maccabbean revolt. Later, the mad emperor Caligula (37-41 AD) demanded to be worshiped as a god and erected a temple to himself in Rome. At his command, the Syrian legate Petronius decided to place a statue of the emperor in the temple in Jerusalem. King Agrippa I succeeded in talking him out of it, but this episode, which had taken place during Paul's lifetime, kept alive the memory of the temple's desecration—an ultimate act of contempt for God.

Scholars are divided over the identity of this man of lawlessness. Some of the language of the passage indicates that the man of lawlessness is a principle—"the secret power of lawlessness" (v6)—rather than a person. This man or principle that "will be revealed" (v8) is "already at work" (v7). "Doomed to destruction" (v3), he opposes God, unlawfully takes a place of worship (v4), and has power that turns out to be counterfeit power "in accordance with the work of Satan" (v9). There is currently one who is "holding him back," but he will be fully revealed (v6), at which time Jesus will destroy him at his Second Coming (v8).

This description is consistent with NT teaching about Satan himself.[1] Already at work in Paul's day, his power is destined to grow. He is at present being restrained, but he will one day be revealed for what he is—and Jesus will return in power to destroy him.

Hebrews 9:27–28: One Life, One Chance

Hebrews 9:27-28 clearly teaches that we are to die and then face judgment. There are no second chances. We will be judged based on how we live life here. There is no purgatory to pray people out of. Death, then judgment—this is the order of things.

James 5:7–9: Be Ready

"The Lord's coming is near....The Judge is standing at the door!" (James 5:8-9). Like Paul writing to the church in Thessalonica, James, the half-brother of Jesus, stresses the imminent return of Jesus. Was James wrong? Obviously not—James was an inspired writer. "The Lord's coming is near" (v8) could refer to the judgment of God upon the city of Jerusalem and first century Judaism. James was the pillar of the church in Jerusalem, which was made up of Jewish Christians. James might have been giving the same warning signs prophesied by Jesus in Mark 13 and Matthew 24, basically, "The judge is at the door, so be ready for judgment."

James teaches the need for patience in light of the imminent judgment of God. If this judgment is soon, then why focus on patience? Why not focus on urgency? Because even though judgment is soon, it will still be a surprise; therefore, there is a need to be ready every day for the coming of Jesus.

2 Peter 3:3–14: All New

Peter, in 2 Peter 3:3-14, gives the same picture of what will occur when Jesus comes as Paul does in Romans 8:17-23. When Jesus comes, a cosmic renewal will occur. God will destroy the present heaven and earth by fire, and he will produce a "new heaven and a new earth." This runs counter to premillennialists who teach that the millennial kingdom will be founded on this earth. The Bible does not teach that Jesus will come twice—once to begin his millennial kingdom and another time to end that kingdom. When Jesus comes, he will come to destroy the earth and begin eternity with a new heaven and a new earth.

1 John 2:18–29, 4:1–6: The Antichrists

The apostle John tackles the issue of the antichrist in 1 John 2:18-29 and 4:1-6. Of first importance is the fact that there is not one all-powerful figure identified as "the Antichrist" in the Scriptures. John mentions here that there are many antichrists; he uses the plural with this term. We need to let him define what he means by the term. He says an antichrist is anyone who denies that Jesus came in the flesh. John was battling a specific false teaching here: Docetism. The Docetists denied the fleshly existence of Jesus; they believed that Jesus only *appeared* to come in the flesh. John says that anyone who accepts this doctrine accepts the teaching of the antichrist.

Contrary to *The Omen* trilogy, this scripture does not teach that a child will be born with 666 blazoned on the back of his neck! Today, premillennialists picture the Antichrist as a figure who will rise up to lead a secret, global government that will form a cashless society and declare war on the church. This makes for nice drama and good horror films, but it's not Biblical. In 1 John the antichrist is anyone who is anti-Jesus—against the fact that Jesus came in the flesh. It is just that simple.

Revelation 20:1–10: The Millennium

This is the one scripture in the Bible that contains the phrase "1000 years" in regard to the reign of Christ. Any discussion of the millennium must consider this passage. Some premillennialists call themselves "one-text premillennialists," believing that if premillennialism is taught in Revelation 20, then that is enough proof for them. If premillennialism were taught in Revelation 20, this would be true because one scripture is enough to support doctrine—but not if your interpretation of the scripture goes counter to what is taught in other scriptures. One principle of Bible interpretation is that less clear passages of Scripture are to be interpreted in light of clearer, more easily understood scriptures. Should we jettison the overall teaching of the Bible concerning the end of time as a result of our interpretation of one highly symbolic, very figurative passage? We will examine this important text and attempt to answer this question in the following chapter.

The Crux of the Matter

Interpreting the Book of Revelation

Having looked at most of the passages of Scripture that are cited to support premillennialism, it is remarkable that not *one* of them mentions a thousand-year reign of Christ. Indeed, the only verses in the entire Bible that refer to a "millennium" are found in the first six verses of Revelation chapter 20. Interpreting and understanding these verses, therefore, is really the crux of the matter. In other words, if Revelation 20:1-10 was unknown, there would be no talk of a thousand-year reign. And if these ten verses of a highly symbolic book do not teach premillennialism, then there is no support for this doctrine in Scripture. In order to "correctly handle" these verses (2 Timothy 2:15), we must first understand their immediate context: the book of Revelation.

Apocalypse Then

As mentioned previously, the last book of the Bible belongs to a genre of literature known as apocalyptic writings. The significance of this simple fact cannot be overstated. Imagine turning on the radio to listen to a baseball game. The announcer intones, "With two men out, it's a three-two pitch; the runner steals a base and now he's on his way home!" There is a sort of code language being used that is readily understood by anyone who follows the game of baseball. However, a visitor from another century, having no knowledge of the sport, would find the words mysterious—or downright incomprehensible. Taken literally, does "two men out" mean that two fellows are unconscious or simply away from their desk at the present time? Does a "three-two pitch" refer to a roof that has a 32-degree slope? Isn't "stealing" wrong? And what is the guy going to do in his house once he reaches "home"? As you can see, the broadcast seems like nonsense if you don't understand the "code language" of the game.

In the same way, the symbols and numbers, images and references of apocalyptic literature may seem strange to us, but they were familiar to their intended audiences in the first century. Once you have a basic grasp of the "game"—in this case the culture of Jewish apocalyptic writings—then the "code language" is easily understood as well.

For instance, numbers in Revelation are often symbolic, as they frequently are throughout the Bible.

- One—unity (one Lord, one faith, one baptism)
- Two—strengthening (Jesus sent out disciples two-by-two)

- Three—divine number (Father, Son and Holy Spirit)
- Four—world or cosmic number (four winds of heaven; four corners of the earth)
- Seven—number of perfection (divine plus cosmic)
- Six—evil and sinister (short of perfect seven, like our thirteen today)
- Three and a half—half of seven, representative of a period of instability and persecution (also referred to as forty-two months, 1260 days, "a time, times and half of a time")
- Ten—completeness (all fingers or toes)
- 1,000—ultimate completeness (10 x 10 x 10)
- Twelve—organized religion (twelve OT tribes, twelve NT apostles)
- 144,000—the full number of all the redeemed of Old and New Testaments (12 x 12 x 1000)

An appreciation of the literary genre allows us to understand a great deal more about the book than you might initially think.

Purpose

The book of Revelation was written by the apostle John to Christians, specifically to seven churches in the Roman province of Asia Minor, part of modern-day Turkey (Revelation 1:4, 2-3). The purpose of the book is stated in the first verse:

The revelation of Jesus Christ, which God gave him to show his servants what must soon take place. He made it known by sending his angel to his servant John. (Revelation 1:1)

There is no need for guesswork, because the book specifically refers to itself as a revelation—or "apocalypse" (the Greek word here is *apokalypsis*). It deals with what would "soon take place" (soon for the first century audience, not for us). The vehicle for the message was a series of visions communicated to John through an angel. All of this is very much in keeping with the methods and purposes of apocalyptic literature. What is more, apocalyptic writing often referred to judgment on a nation or people in language that depicted the end of the world—the end of *their* world, but not the end of *the* world. And every example we have of Jewish apocalyptic literature was written to encourage a persecuted minority to stay true to God, who would ultimately be victorious. This is precisely why Revelation was written.

History Matters

Four basic schools of interpretation have influenced people's views of Revelation. These include:

1. Contemporary Historical (or preterist)—All or almost everything took place in the time when the Revelation was written or shortly thereafter. The symbols don't stand for today's events or persons.

    • Criticism of this method: Passages are written in a vivid style and imagery that often seem to describe scenarios that could only take place at the end of the world. In reality, however, the symbols used in the book were familiar to people in the time they were written.

2. Continuous Historical (or historicist)—Revelation is a blueprint of church history, as advocated by Adam Clark and Albert Barnes. It represents a map of church history from John's day until the end of the world.

   - Criticism of this method: Revelation must mean something to its first readers. As more events transpire in history, this view must continually be updated. Ultimately, a reader would need to know all of the events from Jesus' time until the end of the world in order to understand it.

3. Futurist—Proponents of this method say that most, if not all, of Revelation is yet in the future. This view is necessary if one espouses the teachings of premillennialism. Men such as Hal Lindsey (*The Late Great Planet Earth*) and Tim LaHaye (*Left Behind*) are futurists in their interpretation of Revelation.

   - Criticisms of this method: The message had to mean something to first century readers. It violates Revelation 1:1 and 1:3: "must soon take place" and "the time is near."

4. Symbolic (or idealist)—This method looks at the whole book of Revelation as a drama of historical truths which are not intended for any one generation of Christians, but which are valid over the entire period of church history.

   - Criticisms of this method: Surely there are truths in the book that apply to persecuted disciples in any age.

However, it once more overlooks the meaning for the first century audience.

An understanding of the book simply cannot be divorced from the historical events that prompted its writing. Because of this, a preterist interpretation offers the most reasonable approach.

Date of Writing

Most scholars believe that Revelation describes events that took place during the reign of the Roman emperor Domitian. There is internal evidence, however, that suggests the book was written somewhat earlier. Describing the beast with seven heads, the angel informs John,

> "This calls for a mind with wisdom. The seven heads are seven hills on which the woman sits. They are also seven kings. Five have fallen, one is, the other has not yet come; but when he does come, he must remain for a little while. The beast who once was, and now is not, is an eighth king. He belongs to the seven and is going to his destruction." (Revelation 17:9-11)

Rome was known to all as the city built upon seven hills.[1] The kings then would refer to the Caesars of the Roman Empire, as follows:

1. Augustus   27 BC - 14 AD
2. Tiberius   14-37 AD
3. Caligula   37-41 AD

4. Claudius   41-54 AD
5. Nero   54-68 AD
6. Vespasian   69-79 AD[2]
7. Titus   79-81 AD
8. Domitian   81-96 AD

The book was probably written when the sixth emperor, Vespasian, was on the throne, and it prophesied about the reign of the eighth emperor Domitian. It was written from the Isle of Patmos, where John had been sent to live in exile for his beliefs (Revelation 1:9).

Overview

The book of Revelation can be divided into seven sections, most of which refer to events that took place in the first century AD. The very end of the book describes events at the end of time, assuring us of God's ultimate victory by offering a glimpse of the final judgment, heaven and hell. In outline form,[3] we have:

1. Prologue (chapter 1)
2. Letters to the Seven Churches (2-3)
3. John has the vision of the presence of God (4-5)
4. The book of destiny is opened as we glimpse the coming terrible events connected with the day of the Lord (6-18).
   a. The opening of the seven seals (6:1-17).
   b. Seven trumpets blast and each successive blast produces a new terror (8:1-13, 9:1-21, 11:15-19).

    c. Seven bowls, each pouring out dreadful things (16:1-21).

    d. War in heaven and the Devil is cast out and comes to earth (12).

    e. The beast comes and does his terrible work (13).

5. Final defeat of the beast (19:19-21) and the thousand-year reign of martyred saints (20:1-6)

6. The conflict to end all conflicts. The Devil is flung into the lake of fire and then the general resurrection and the final judgment (20:7-15)

7. Picture of a new heaven and the new earth and a picture of the New Jerusalem (21:1-22:5)

Millennium

Against this backdrop, we come at last to Revelation chapter 20. Having described the downfall of the beast and its allies (representing various aspects of the Roman Empire) in chapter 19, John now gives us a glimpse of the bigger picture: the ultimate defeat and demise of Satan.

In verses 1-3, Satan is bound with a great chain for a thousand years "to keep him from deceiving the nations." Certainly the elements of this description are not meant to be taken literally. The "chain" is not a literal chain, but rather it indicates a significant curtailing or limiting of Satan's powers. Similarly, the thousand years is not an exact span of years, but is a number that symbolizes ultimate completeness (10 x 10 x 10)—that is, the devil will be bound for a very long time.

When does this binding take place? Verses 4-6 offer some help here. John now describes a "first resurrection" of martyred saints who "came to life and reigned with Christ a thousand years." These are the souls first mentioned at the opening of the fifth seal (Revelation 6:9-11), who were "under the altar"—*in heaven*. They reign with Jesus who is also reigning right now *in heaven*.[4] In terminology similar to Ezekiel 37, this "first resurrection" is the resurrection of *their cause*. Their questioning plea to God had been "How long...?" (Revelation 6:10). God does not forget them, but upholds their cause until "the rest of the dead" come to life at the end of the millennium.

The New Testament consistently teaches that there will be one bodily resurrection at the last day.[5] Since Jesus will reign from heaven until the resurrection of the dead at the end of the thousand years, and since he is even now reigning from heaven we can conclude that the millennium began when Jesus returned to heaven and will continue until he comes again. The millennium is underway right now! The premillennialist's claim of *multiple* bodily resurrections, separated by a literal thousand year reign *on earth* of Christ and his saints, simply does not line up with Scripture.

Verses 7-10 describe what will happen next. When the "thousand years" have ended, Satan will be released "for a short time" (v3), unrestricted in his capacity to deceive the nations once again. Perhaps this has something to do with his ability to coordinate a worldwide persecution, something unheard of since the fall of the Roman Empire. But God will intervene at the end of time and cast Satan into the lake of fire, at which time the dead will rise for judgment. No one can withstand the mighty purposes of God, who will be victorious in the end!

N

The remainder of Revelation goes on to recount events that will occur at the end of the world: the final judgment and unhindered eternal life with God. The millennium, then, is the period of time between Christ's first and second comings—in other words, the church age. This interpretation of Revelation is not only Biblically sound and coherent, but takes into account the historical events that prompted its writing in the first place. The book gave great assurance and hope to Christians who were undergoing very real persecution in the first century.

Revelation is not a book to be feared. When understood in its historical and literary context, its exhortation to persevere and its promise of God's ultimate triumph in the world can encourage readers in any century.

How Should We Then Live?

Like a Thief in the Night

For you know very well that the day of the Lord will come like a thief in the night.

1 Thessalonians 5:2

Biblical teaching about the end of time should inspire us to take a closer look at how we are living in the here and now. These teachings were not given to create dramatic end-time predictions about a demonic political leader and a new world order. This may sell books, but it isn't Biblical. Rather, God wants us to reflect on how we are living our lives. What can we discover about the here and now by taking a look at the hereafter? Let's look at a few lessons that we can learn.

Jesus Is Coming Like a Thief

But we, wholly ignorant of the future and very imperfectly informed about the past, cannot tell at what moment the end ought to come. That it will come when it ought, we may be sure; but we waste our time in guessing when that will be. That it has a meaning we may be sure, but we cannot see it. When it is over, we may be told.[1]

C. S. Lewis, literary critic and writer

The verdict of history seems clear. Great spiritual gain comes from living under the expectation of Christ's return. But wisdom and restraint are also in order. At the very least, it would be well for those in our age who predict details and dates for the End to remember how many before them have misread the signs of the times.

Mark Noll, religious writer

In the Spring of 1978 while I was in college, I took a road trip from West Tennessee across the Mississippi River to St. Louis, Missouri, with my roommate, Barry, to watch three games between the St. Louis Cardinals and the Los Angeles Dodgers. I was a Dodger fan in the heyday of Steve Garvey and Ron Cey. Barry loved Lou Brock and the Cards. The Dodgers took two out of three that weekend on the Cardinals' home field—I felt really good about that!

After one game Barry and I stood over the top of the parking lot, looking out over Busch Field. Bright lights on a baseball diamond is a magical sight. Below us, hundreds of fans were streaming from the ball park to their cars. Not being disciples, and just to give them something to talk about on their ride home, Barry and I began to shout, "Repent, the world is coming to an end! Repent! Repent! Time is short! Repent!" People passed by underneath hearing voices from the sky informing them that the world was going to end soon. They probably filed the information in the category of "Stupid Things You Should Not Pay Attention To." That's where I would have filed it.

But at the dawn of a new millennium, many voices have once again been pounding the airwaves to tell us that the world is going to end soon. They beckon us to repent, for the end of time is near. Where do we file this information?

Millennial Madness

As 1999 drew to a close, many prophets of doom were busy announcing from the mountaintops that the world was about to end. The end they predicted was to come in a variety of ways— the Y2K computer crisis, a lethal virus released on humanity by an angry Mother Nature, the return of an extraterrestrial or the Second Coming of Jesus.

My family had the opportunity to live in Israel from August 1997 to August 1998. During this time I met many people who had moved to Israel for the year 2000. They were anticipating the return of the Messiah, and they wanted to be at ground zero when he came. Ground zero, for much of the religious world, is the Mount of Olives, overlooking the Temple Mount in Jerusalem. Since Jesus' sky-gazing disciples were told that he "will come back in the same way you have seen him go into heaven" (Acts 1:11), many evangelical Christians have taken this to mean that he will return to the place where he left: the Mount of Olives.

One person who believes this gathered together a handful of devoted followers and set up camp on the Mount of Olives. He called himself "David." No one is sure if that was his real name

Guess I Missed Again...

Throughout the centuries, many have predicted the return of Jesus. So far, no one has been right. Maybe the scriptures which speak about Jesus coming like a thief in the night should be given more thought by prognosticators wishing to predict the time of his return (Matthew 24:36). Here is a list of some dates that have been set for Jesus' Second Coming and the people who predicted them.

Date	Person
c. 210 AD	Hippolytus, early church father and a bishop of Rome.
1260	Joachim of Fiore, a Catholic monk.
1420	The Taborite sect in Bohemia.
	Thomas Müntzer, leader of a German sect.
June 18, 1666	Shabbetai Zevi, a Cabalist Jew who declared himself to be the Messiah. On September 15, 1666, he converted to Islam.
	John Napier, a Scottish writer.
1694	Johann Heinrich Alsted (1588-1638), a reformed theologian.
	Thomas Beverly, Pierre Jurieu, Richard Clarke, Edward King and Richard Valpy, J. A. Bengel
March 21, 1844	William Miller, founder of the Seventh-Day Adventists. This date is known as the First Disappointment in Adventist history.
October 22, 1844	Miller's followers predict the return of Jesus for a second time. This date is known as the Great Disappointment.
	J. P. Petri, Joseph Lathrop, John Gill, Samuel Hopkins.
1873, 1874, 1878	Nelson H. Barbour, an Adventist who influenced Charles Taze Russell, the founder of the Jehovah's Witnesses. Barbour tried at least three times to predict the date of Jesus' return.
1874	Charles Taze Russell's first attempt to predict the return of Jesus.
1878	Russell's second attempt to predict the return of Jesus.
October 1914	Elliott Kamwana, a preacher in the Southeast African territory of Nyasaland.

1914	Russell's third guess.
1915	Russell's fourth and last attempt to predict the end of the world. He died in 1916.
1918	Joseph F. Rutherford, successor to Russell as the second president of the Jehovah's Witnesses, predicts this date.
1925	Christabel Pankhurst, one of the few women writers to enter the field of end-time prognosticators. Rutherford tries again and misses.
April 25, 1959	Florence Houteff, early leader of the Branch Davidians.
1954, 1975	Other dates selected by the Jehovah's Witnesses for the Second Coming of Jesus. They haven't selected another date since 1975.
Sept. 11-13, 1988	Edgar Whisenant, writer of the two-million-copy best-seller *88 Reasons Why the Rapture Will Be in 1988.*
1988	Hal Lindsey, author of *The Late Great Planet Earth.*
Oct. 28, 1992	The Mission for the Coming Days in Flushing, N.Y.
Sept. 6, 1994	Harold Camping, author of *1994*. On September 7 he reevaluates and sets September 29 as the correct date.
Sept. 29, 1994	Camping misses again.
Oct. 2, 1994	Camping misses again.
March 31, 1995	Camping misses again. After the fourth try, Camping stops making predictions.
Sept. 17, 2001	Current pyramidologists, who study the Great Pyramid of Giza to ascertain the date of the Rapture.
Dec. 31, 2011	Solara, a New Age leader. (He says that this date can be avoided if people choose to attain a higher consciousness before the day arrives.)

or not. I had the opportunity to meet David one day while walking around the Jewish Quarter of the Old City of Jerusalem. A shop owner pointed him out to me. David and I had this conversation:

I asked, "David, why are you living in a tent on the Mount of Olives?"

Prognosticators Aplenty

Besides your everyday dispensational premillennialist, prognosticators come in many other kinds and flavors. Here are a few:

Nostradamus
Edgar Cayce, "The Sleeping Prophet"
Tea leaf readers
Palm readers
Tarot card readers
Astrologers
Fortune cookies
Crystal ball readers
People who communicate with extraterrestrials
James Redfield, *The Celestine Prophesy*
Native American spiritualists
Channelers

"Because Jesus is coming back soon," he replied.

I asked, "How do you know this?"

He said, "The signs are all around us—wars and rumors of wars, famine, pestilence—all the signs are there."

"But those signs have always been there, and people have been predicting the Lord's return for centuries. What do you think about the scripture in which Jesus says he will come as a thief?" I asked.

"I prefer to look at the scriptures that show when he is coming," David answered.

I said, "But if he comes as a thief, he won't tip his cards and let you know when he is coming."

David said, "He's already tipped his cards. Expect him to land on the Mount of Olives on January 1, 2000."

David walked away to await the coming of Jesus. If the Israeli government hasn't moved him off the Mount, then for all I know, he may still be there waiting for Jesus to appear.

The Inside Scoop

The absolute number one problem that I have with dispensational premillennialists and end-of-the-world soothsayers is their arrogance in acting as if they know something that even Jesus himself said he did not know. Jesus said that he did not know the day or the hour that the Father had set for his coming. "No one knows about that day or hour, not even the angels in heaven, nor the Son, but only the Father" (Matthew 24:36). If Jesus does not know the time, then why would any mere mortal claim to know when the Lord is coming and the world will end? What arrogance on the part of anyone who would make such a claim! And yet dozens of people throughout history—and even today—continue to make predictions about when the world will end.

Jesus will come like a thief. He will come unannounced. He will surprise us. Therefore, we must be vigilant. We must stay awake and keep watch. We must be ready always for the coming of the Messiah.

Seize the Day

And now, dear children, continue in him, so that when he appears we may be confident and unashamed before him at his coming.

1 John 2:28

Reading what premillennial dispensationalists have written can be very confusing. The Bible is a book that is meant to clarify life. To be sure, there are difficult concepts in the Scriptures, and no one can ever fully understand the mind of God; however, God is not a God of confusion, but of peace. Premillennial doctrine is confusing. People can spend so much time studying the intensity of earthquakes, proposing the identity of the Antichrist and offering conjectures about the mark of the beast that they can lose focus on why they have been called to follow Jesus—to make other disciples.

As disciples, we need to realize that we will not be judged on how well we understand the doctrine of the end-time, but rather on how we lived our lives. When we stand before the judgment seat of God, we will not be questioned about the meaning of the 144,000 in Revelation. It's useful for us to know something about these matters because false doctrine is often built around them here on earth. Since people can be sucked into and destroyed by false doctrine, we need to know how to disprove it.

Rather than quizzing ourselves on what we know about Revelation, we need to be asking questions like the following: What am I doing as a disciple right now to make a difference in the world right where I live? Am I touching the life of someone around me, making an eternal difference? What am I doing as a parent to make sure that my children make it to heaven? Does my marriage draw people to the church? Are my friendships in the Lord making the gospel attractive to my friends in the world?

These questions meet life where we live it—in the here and now. Any discussion about the end of time should direct us to questions about how we are living life in the here and now.

Your Last Day

He who loves the coming of the Lord is not he who affirms it is far off, nor is it he who says it is near. It is he who, whether it be far or near, awaits it with sincere faith, steadfast hope, and fervent love.

Augustine of Hippo, theologian

For to me, to live is Christ and to die is gain.

Paul, Philippians 1:21

What if this present were the world's last night?
Holy Sonnets XIII
John Donne, poet and minister

We must never speak to simple, excitable people about "the Day" without emphasizing again and again the utter impossibility of prediction. We must try to show them that that impossibility is an essential part of the doctrine. If you do not believe our Lord's words, why do you believe in his return at all? And if you do believe them must you not put away from you, utterly and forever, any hope of dating that return? His teaching on the subject quite clearly consisted of three propositions. (1) That he will certainly return. (2) That we cannot possibly find out when. (3) And that therefore we must always be ready for him.[1]
C. S. Lewis, literary critic and author

I heard a joke once that went something like this: A doctor called up a patient and said, "I've got good news and I've got bad news. Which do you want to hear first?"

The patient said, "Please, give me the good news first."

The doctor replied, "Okay, you have twenty-four hours left to live."

The patient quickly responded, "That's the good news—I have twenty-four hours left to live? Then what is the bad news?"

The doctor answered, "I should have called you yesterday!"

What if you knew that you only had twenty-four hours left to live? What would you do differently? Would you make sure that each moment was lived to the fullest? Would you tell your family and friends how much you appreciate them? Would you finally apologize for that wrong that you committed years ago? How would this type of news change you?

The Bible teaches that we should live each day, each moment, like it is our last. James tells us that life is like steam that rises from the boiling pot and vanishes in the air (James 4:14). We are here for a short time, then we are gone. Not even the next minute is guaranteed. Right now, stop for a moment and think about this: If I had one more day, what would I do with it? Then— go do it! Tell your wife how much you love her. Hug your children extra hard. Be open about hidden sin. If you haven't been baptized, find someone to dunk you. Live life like it has an expiration date, because in truth, *it does.*

Give It Your Best

People get ready, there's a train a-comin',
You don't need no ticket, you just get on board.
All you need is faith to hear the diesels hummin'
Don't need no ticket, you just thank the Lord.

"People Get Ready"
Curtis Mayfield, 1964

According to the book of Hebrews, "It is appointed unto men once to die, but after this the judgment" (Hebrews 9:27, KJV). This means no second chance. Reincarnation is not an option. After death you don't come back as a grasshopper or a python or a member of the Kennedy family or a talk show host. The soul does not transmigrate—it goes to God and awaits judgment.

Also, purgatory is not in the picture. Souls are not held in limbo while the prayers of those left behind determine their fates. No matter how many candles are lit for the dearly departed, their place in eternity will not change. We don't get a second chance.

Also, "baptism for the dead" is ineffective. In Salt Lake City, people get dunked in water dozens of times for their family members who died before them. This might comfort their own minds, but it has no power on those who have passed on to the next world. We get one chance—one shot—no second try. You live, you die, then judgment.

This being the case, we need to give everything we have toward making our lives count. In a basketball game, if you have the ball with six seconds on the clock and you are down by a point, what do you do? You call time-out. You get the coaches and the players together and you map out what you think will be the best play to score. You try to get the ball to your best ball handler, your best scorer, your go-to man.

I'll never forget the last shot that Michael Jordan ever took in the NBA. Down by a point with little time left on the clock, he dribbled to the top of the key, faked right and pushed off ever so slightly on Bryon Russell. He then stepped left, floated up in the air and sent the ball heading toward the basket. As soon as the ball left the tips of his fingers, he knew that it is good. He left his hand in the air as the ball sailed through the rim, through the net and down toward the floor. He backpedaled with this hand still in the air, showing the graceful follow-through that made him the NBA's leading scorer season after season. The scene looked like it had been scripted for a movie. If you find your team down with six seconds on the clock, you want Jordan on your team and the ball in his hand.

We need to live every moment of every day as though we have six seconds left to play and we are down by one point. This is impossible to do in reality, but it must be what we strive to do. Only one person ever lived his life with this degree of intensity: Jesus of Nazareth. Jesus was a man of purpose. His head was always in the game. He never forfeited an opportunity to do good. He never wasted a moment. He was always serving, always teaching, always a perfect example, always focused on doing what was right. He lived this way with a graceful, calming charm. At times he would nap, but he woke from his naps ready to get to work. He would take time to be by himself only so that he could recharge and get back to the people. He was never frantic, never worried, never out of control, never overwrought. He lived each moment of every day to its fullest. He is the example of how we need to approach life. We must live like there are six seconds left to play and we are down by one point. Your number has been called and the ball is in your hand. What are you going to do?

An Outline of the Book of Revelation

Chapters 1–3: Prologue and the Seven Churches

1:1-4: Prologue

1:5-8: Greeting

1:9-20: John's vision—sees one like a Son of Man with seven stars, which are the seven angels of the seven churches; seven lampstands, which are the seven churches

2:1-7: Ephesus—center of worship of Artemis.

    a. Commendation: Their labor, patience, doctrinal strictness and orthodoxy. They were against false teachers and the Nicolaitans (vv4-5).

    b. Condemnation: Forsaking of their first love—"Remember the height from which you have fallen" (v5).

    c. Appeal: Remember, repent, do.

2:8-11: Smyrna—fairest city of Ionia; center of Paganism; large Jewish population that was hostile to Christians, referred to here as the "synagogue of Satan," was persecuting them.

    a. Commendation: Endured persecution and poverty.

    b. Condemnation: None.

    c. Appeal: Stay faithful unto death, and you will receive a crown of life from Jesus.

2:12-17: Pergamum—provincial capital, located in the southern part of Myria; site of a famous library which first developed parchment because the Alexandrian library, their rival, stopped sending them papyrus; center of paganism and emperor worship. [*Author's note:* There's a great display of the altar of Pergamum at the Metropolitan Museum in New York.]

    a. Commendation: Remained true to Jesus' name; didn't deny the faith during persecution.

    b. Condemnation: Held to the false teaching of Balaam and Nicolaitans.

    c. Appeal: "Repent" (v16).

2:18-29: Thyatira—noted for its red or purple dyes; more trade guilds here than in any other city.

    a. Commendation: Increased their deeds for God as time went by.

    b. Condemnation: Tolerated the woman Jezebel. Probably not her real name, but an influential woman having a negative influence.

    c. Appeal: "Hold on" (v25).

3:1-6: Sardis—wealthy, degenerate, proud city; held a position that was almost impregnable from military assault but had twice fallen due to carelessness, hence, "wake up" carries extra meaning.

    a. Commendation: None.

    b. Condemnation: Had a reputation of being alive, but they were dead.

    c. Appeal: "Wake up" (v2).

3:7-13: Philadelphia—built as a gateway to the East to spread Greek culture.

    a. Commendation: Kept his commands.

    b. Condemnation: None.

    c. Appeal: Keep persevering.

3:14-22: Laodicea—center of banking, wool manufacture and medicine.

  a. Commendation: None.

  b. Condemnation: Lukewarm—nauseating to the Lord; self-deceived; enjoyed a false security.

  c. Appeal: Repent!

Chapters 4–6: The Throne, the Lamb and the Six Seals

Chapter 4: The Throne

4:1-6: A throne in heaven surrounded by twenty-four other thrones on which sat twenty-four elders.

4:6-8: Four living creatures—lion, ox, man, flying eagle—with six wings and eyes all around saying, "Holy, Holy, Holy." These are extensions of God: Lion stands for strength and bravery; calf stands for service; man stands for wisdom; eagle stands for swiftness.

4:9-11: Elders bow before the throne.

Chapter 5: Worthy Is the Lamb

5:1-5: Scroll with seven seals—both sides of the scroll suggests a very full revelation concerning the destiny of men faced by visitations of God's wrath. "Wept much" because of the great importance of the message; "Lion of the tribe" represents the noblest son.

5:6-8: The Lamb takes the scroll. The lion represents absolute strength and bravery. Lamb is a religious symbol representing sacrifice. Both are used as symbols for Jesus. The seven horns stand for strength and honor; seven eyes stand for Christ's vigilance.

5:8: Golden bowls full of incense are the prayers of the saints.

5:9-14: Praise to the Lamb.

Chapter 6: Six Seals Are Opened

6:1-ff: Opens the seals on the scroll.

6:1-2: First seal sends forth a white horse, a conqueror bent on conquest, which stands for the preaching of the gospel.

6:3-4: Second seal sends forth a fiery red horse, the power to take peace from the earth; bloodshed and war show that persecution closely follows the preaching of the gospel.

6:5-6: Third seal sends forth a black horse with a pair of scales in the rider's hand, standing for economic discrimination against Christians.

6:7-8: Fourth seal sends forth a pale horse (the color of a corpse) with a rider named Death, with the power to kill one-fourth of the population of the earth. Death and Hades follow persecution.

6:9-11: Fifth seal reveals the martyrs; John asks, "How long until they will be avenged?"

6:12-17: Sixth seal opening causes a great earthquake, along with the sun turning black, the moon turning red, stars falling to the earth, and every mountain and island being removed, all of which stands for a day of God's wrath (v17)—judgment by natural calamity.

Chapter 7: The Servants

Chapter 7: Interlude Between Seals

7:1-8 4: Angels who hold back the four winds are told not to harm the earth until the 144,000 are sealed.

7:9-17: A multitude in white robes before the throne stands for those washed in the blood of the Lamb, Jesus.

7:16-17: The saved will never hunger or thirst and there will be no tears. 144,000 stands for the redeemed of all ages, Jew and Gentile.

Chapters 8-9: The Seventh Seal—Sound the Trumpets

8:1-5: Opening of the seventh seal produces silence in heaven for a half hour. The silence stands for the calm before the storm. Then seven angels with seven trumpets appear. An angel with a golden censer offered incense, which represents the prayers of the saints in 5:8. Incense added to the prayers suggests strength, showing that Christ and the Holy Spirit help in intercession. The incense and censer of fire show that God hears and responds with judgments. He throws fire from the altar to the earth.

8:6-ff: Angels and their trumpets.

8:7: First angel/trumpet brings hail and fire mixed with blood, burning one-third of the earth and trees and all the grass—a warning sign.

8:8-9: Second angel/trumpet brings a mountain of fire thrown into the sea; a third of the sea is turned into blood; a third of living sea creatures die; and a third of ships are destroyed. The mountain being moved suggests great trouble (mountains are a symbol of strength).

8:10-11: Third angel/trumpet brings a blazing star which falls on a third of the rivers and springs. The name of star is Wormwood. A third of the water turns bitter. A great star fallen suggests a great power that lost its position.

8:12: Fourth angel/trumpet blacks out a third of the sun, moon and stars, and a third of the day and night are without light.

8:13: Eagle announces woes will be coming with the next three trumpets. The woes represent three remaining trumpets that will be worse in their effect than the previous ones.

9:1-6: Fifth angel/trumpet brings a star which opened the Abyss. Smoke darkens the sky and locusts come out with the power of scorpions. Told to harm those without the seal of God on their foreheads, they torture them for five months. The Abyss is the place where demons reside. Since smoke blocks true light, this symbol represents the false doctrine that Satan is promoting. Locusts are a dreaded plague, portraying the judgment of God. In this case the locust plague portrays a judgment against Rome through internal decay.

9:7-11: Describes the locusts as battle horses with human faces.

9:11: The angel of the Abyss has a Hebrew name—Abaddon—and a Greek name—Apollyon, both meaning Destroyer.

9:13-21: Sixth angel/trumpet rallies four angels to kill a third of mankind and to gather 200 million troops.

9:17-19: Describes the horses and riders (troops), which are symbolic of great destruction and judgment, with heads like a lions and spewing fire, smoke and sulfur. Their tails are like snakes.

9:20-21: The rest of humanity still does not repent. (The purpose of the judgment is to induce repentance.) The voice from the horns of the altar represents the prayers of saints for the next judgment.

Chapter 10: The Scroll

10:1-11: An angel who stands on land and sea, delivers the universal message. The lion roaring suggests a not-so-happy message. Sealing it up means that no more warning will be given. Eating the scroll means that the message is to be completely digested. The eaten scroll was sweet to the mouth and sour to the stomach. It was sweet because it was the precious word of God and sour because of the warnings and judgments it contained.

Chapter 11: The Witnesses and the Seventh Trumpet

11:1-6: Temple being measured shows God's protection for his people. Forty-two months is equal to three-and-a-half years, which stands for a period of persecution—i.e. an unstable number, perhaps showing inadequate efforts to defeat the church. Two witnesses testify for God—olive trees and candlesticks, a continual supply of the Spirit for the preaching.

11:7-14: The beast attacks the two witnesses and kills them, referring to the apparent success of Roman persecution.

11:15-19: Seventh angel/trumpet (the last trumpet) would normally indicate that the time for the last judgment has come, as announced by the twenty-four elders.

Chapter 12: The Woman, the Dragon and the Child

12:1-2: Woman clothed with the sun appears in heaven, crying out with birth pains.

12:3-4: An enormous red dragon with seven heads and ten horns and seven crowns. His tails sweep away a third of the stars. He waits to eat the newborn child. Red stands for the color of blood. The seven heads stand for great wisdom. The ten horns represent great power. The seven diadems stand for great authority. The dragon's purpose is to devour the child.

12:5-6: The woman gives birth to a son who is snatched up by God.

12:7-9: There is war in heaven. Michael is the protector of God's people. Satan falling from heaven stands for the limiting of his power. This does not show the origin of Satan or his literal casting out of heaven; these signify his defeat by Christ.

12:10-12: The devil is filled with fury.

12:13-17: The dragon pursues the woman who gave birth. She is given wings like an eagle to flee from him, which symbolizes the church fleeing from persecution. Since he cannot catch her, he wages war on her offspring—the Christians.

Chapter 13–16: The 144,000 and the Bowls of Wrath

Chapter 13: The Sea Beast and Land Beast, Two of Satan's Allies

13:1-2: The beast of the sea has seven heads, ten horns and ten crowns and each had a blasphemous name written on its head. The blasphemy stands for the Roman emperor's claims of divinity. One head smitten but healed stands for Nero's death (the first emperor to persecute Christians), and the healed wound refers to Nero-like persecution which resumed under Domitian (81-96 AD), like a leopard with feet of a bear and mouth of a lion. Combining characteristics of several animals draws a picture of the epitome of a worldly, tyrannical empire—the swiftness and stealth of the leopard with the strength of the bear and the fearlessness of the lion.

13:3-4: Men worship the dragon and the beast.

13:5-10: The beast makes war against humankind.

13:10: The war calls for patient endurance by the saints.

13:11-18: The beast out of the earth has two horns like a lamb and speaks like the dragon, and it makes people worship the beast of the sea. The mark on the hand or the forehead stands for physical service or intellectual service to the emperor.

13:17: The mark of 666 used the number six, which was just short of perfect seven and could mean "failure upon failure." Six was a sinister, evil number, so the mark may stand for evil raised to its highest power, referring to the anti-Christian Roman system.

Chapter 14: The 144,000

14:1-5: The Lamb, Jesus, is standing on Mt. Zion with the 144,000, the redeemed of all ages, learning a new song.

14:4-5: The 144,000 are described as men, virgins, martyrs, blameless and those who never lied.

14:6-7: First angel, with the eternal gospel, says, "Fear God."

14:8 Second angel says, "Fallen is Babylon the Great," a veiled reference to Rome.

14:9 Third angel says, "Woe to those with the mark of the beast," those who are not Christians.

14:12: Saints need to have patient endurance through these trials.

14:14-16: The Son of Man sits on a cloud with sickle in his hand, harvesting the earth. In the apocalyptic tradition of the Gospels, the Son of Man comes seated on a cloud to judge the earth. The sickle represents the harvesting of God's people from the world. John is encouraging the disciples to endure the persecution because God will pronounce them righteous. But what will happen to those not claimed by God?

14:17-20: An angel harvests grapes that are put in the winepress of God's wrath, meaning that God's wrath will be revealed to all who have not obeyed him. John also encourages the disciples by noting that God's wrath will be poured out on any who do not acknowledge Jesus.

Chapter 15: Introduction to the Bowls

15:1-4: The wrath of God is finished. The hope of repentance for the unrighteous is past. Those victorious over the beast sing praise to God.

15:5-8: Seven angels with seven plagues appear.

Chapter 16: The Bowls

16:1-2: First angel poured a bowl on the land. Painful sores broke out on those with the mark of the beast.

16:3: Second angel poured a bowl on the sea, which turned to blood and everything in it died.

16:4-7: Third angel poured a bowl over rivers and springs and they became blood.

16:9: Fourth angel poured a bowl on the sun, and the sun scorched people with fire. The first four plagues attack four elements of the physical world—the land, various bodies of water and people.

16:10-11: Fifth angel poured a bowl over the throne of the beast and his kingdom was plunged into darkness.

16:12-14: Sixth angel poured a bowl over the great river Euphrates and the water dried up. Three demons that looked like frogs came from the mouth of the dragon, representing unclean spirits or evil propaganda to deceive other nations into helping. They gathered kings for battle.

16:16: Kings gathered at Armageddon, symbolizing righteousness and evil locked in deadly combat. It is a spiritual battle, not a physical one.

The next two plagues attack the kingdoms of the world—the nations and the leaders of those nations.

16:17: Seventh angel poured a bowl into the air. A voice came from the throne, "It is done." A great earthquake split the city into three parts. Hailstones weighing a hundred pounds each fell on humanity. The last plague symbolizes that God has finished judging the world. "It is done," hearkens back to the last words of Jesus on the cross: "It is finished." God will now proceed to pronounce judgment upon Satan and his minions.

Chapters 17–19: The Prostitute, the Beasts and the Fall of Babylon

Chapter 17: The Scarlet Woman As Worldly Rome

17:1-6: The adulterous woman who was drunk with blood of the saints, or Babylon the Great, the mother of prostitutes, stands for the worldliness of Rome. The scarlet-colored beast suggests that it is covered in sin. "Sitting on the beast" stands for political Rome supporting worldly Rome, the prostitute. The cup of abominations shows how worldliness looks attractive, but the results are despicable.

17:6-8: The beast reflects the emperor worship; next in line is Domitian, the next great persecutor of the church.

17:9: The seven heads represent the seven hills on which the woman sits. Rome is built on seven hills.

17:10-11: The kings represent Roman emperors. Five have already fallen. "One who is" refers to Vespasian. The one to come for a little while is Titus. Then the eighth is Domitian.

17:12-14: The ten horns represent ten kings.

17:18: The woman is the great city of Rome that rules over the earth.

Chapter 18: The Fall of Babylon the Great

18:1-3: A splendid angel announces the "fall of Babylon," the impending fall of Rome.

18:4-8: Another voice talks about the fall.

18:9-20: Kings, merchants and sea captains all grieve over Babylon because of the loss of their own profits.

18:21-24: Another angel announces the fall.

Chapter 19: The Beast and False Prophet Destroyed

19:1-3: A great multitude in heaven, the redeemed, shouts praise for the condemning of the great prostitute, Rome.

19:4-10: The multitude is praising the wedding of the Lamb and his bride, Jesus and his church.

19:11-16: The resurrected Lord rides in triumph.

19:17-18: An angel standing in the sun calls to the birds to eat the flesh of humanity. This image seems to imply that God is ready to pass judgment upon all of humanity.

19:19-21: The outcome of the spiritual battle between good and evil is seen in the final doom of the beast and false prophet. The beast and his army make war against the rider. The beast and false prophet are captured and thrown in the fiery lake, and the rest of the army is killed with the sword of the Rider. Thus the prostitute, beast and false prophet (allies of Satan) have all been destroyed. In chapter 20, the Devil himself will be destroyed.

Chapters 20–22 Satan Bound and Defeated; Heaven Begins

Chapter 20: The Defeat of Satan and the Final Judgment

20:1-3: An angel has the key to the Abyss. Chaining the dragon represents chaining Satan, who would be locked in the Abyss for a thousand years, a long period of time. His binding means that he will be limited in some manner or to some degree by the work of Christ, but he won't be totally incapacitated.

20:4-6: Thrones are provided for the judges, and those beheaded for God come to life and reign for a thousand years, a long time.

20:7-10: Satan is released after a long period of time, and he declares war on the city of God, the church. At the close of this period, then, Satan will be free for a short time to once again deceive nations, probably a reference to a time of persecution on a large scale. God defeats him, his followers are consumed in fire, and Satan himself is thrown into the Abyss with the beast and the false prophet to be tormented forever and ever.

20:11-15: The Resurrection, after which all the dead are judged by what they had done. Anyone's name not found in the "Book of life" is thrown in the fiery lake. Heaven and earth are destroyed; the physical universe is gone. There is one bodily resurrection and one judgment of all men, good and evil. All are raised in the same "hour." The righteous are raised at the "last day," and the wicked are judged at the last day.

Chapter 21-22 The Destiny of the Redeemed—Heaven Begins

21:1-6: New Jerusalem comes down from heaven. God wipes away every tear and makes everything new.

21:8: List of sins of those who will go to the fiery lake, called the second death.

21:9-14: The New Jerusalem shines like a precious jewel. The high wall has twelve gates, each named for a tribe of Israel. The twelve foundations are named for the twelve apostles. The redeemed of the Old Testament and New Testament will be with God in heaven.

21:15-21: The city is described like a square, walls are of jasper, the city of pure gold, clear as glass. Heaven defies our ability to describe it.

21:22-27: The Glory of God gives it light; there will be no night there.

21:27: Nothing impure will enter it.

22:1-5: The river of life flows from God's throne down the middle of the great street. The tree of life will be on each side of the river. The twelve crops of fruit each month describe the never-ending abundance of life with God in heaven.

22:6: These words are true.

22:7: Jesus is coming soon; therefore, keep these words.

22:8-11: John is told to keep the book open, for these things will happen.

22:15: Sins are listed.

22:18-19: A warning about adding to or taking from this book is issued.

Last words of Revelation 22:

    1. Last blessing (v14).

    2. Last invitation (v17).

    3. Last warning (vv18-19).

    4. Last promise (v20).

    5. Last prayer (v20).

Notes

Chapter 1—Fever Pitch

1. From the official Web site of the *Left Behind* series (www.leftbehind.com/book_series.html), July 19, 2000.

Chapter 3—Three Millennial Theories

1. Others in the amillennialist camp hold that the events described in Revelation refer to the destruction of the Jewish temple in 70 AD or to the persecution of Christians under Nero after the great fire of Rome in 64 AD. However, internal evidence suggests that the persecution during the reign of Domitian (81-96 AD) was most likely in view. See chapter 10 and the appendix for details.

2. C. S. Lewis, *The World's Last Night and Other Essays* (New York: Harcourt, Brace, and Co., 1960) 100-101.

Chapter 5—What's Wrong with This Picture?

1. Charles Ryrie, *Dispensationalism Today* (Chicago: Moody Press, 1965), 45.

2. Loraine Boettner, *The Meaning of the Millennium: Four Views*, ed. Robert G. Clouse (Downers Grove, Illinois: InterVarsity Press, 1977), 52-53.

Chapter 6—A Profusion of Confusion

1. Lewis, *The World's Last Night,* 93.

2. See Matthew 24:42, 25:13, Acts 1:7, Colossians 2:16-19, 1 Thessalonians 5:2, 1 John 3:2 and Revelation 10:7.

3. 1 Thessalonians 5:2, 2 Peter 3:10 and Revelation 3:3 and 16:15.

Chapter 7—Old Testament Verses

1. Mark 1:15, 9:1; Colossians 1:13 and Revelation 1:6, 9.

Chapter 8—New Testament Verses

1. Other possibilities that have been put forth for the identity of the "man of lawlessness" and the force that restrains him include: (1) the

predisposition of Roman emperors to demand worship, as seen in Caligula (37-41 AD), being held in check temporarily by Claudius (41-54 AD), but to be seen again in emperors such as Nero and Domitian; (2) Jewish persecution in the first century, being restrained by the Roman Empire; (3) a personal Antichrist who will be restrained for a time by the government (premillennial); and (4) the Roman Catholic Church being restrained by law and morality (postmillennial).

Chapter 9—The Crux of the Matter

1. The seven hills were Palatine, Capitoline, Quirinal, Viminal, Esquiline, Caelian and Aventine.

2. The period of instability that followed Nero's death saw a succession of three men who were declared "emperor" in the space of a year. None however gained the allegiance of the entire Roman Empire until Vespasian. They were Galba (Oct. 68-Jan 69 AD), Otho (Jan-Mar 69 AD) and Vitellius (June-Dec 69 AD).

3. See the appendix for an expanded outline, and Gordon Ferguson's *Mine Eyes Have Seen the Glory* (Woburn, Mass.: DPI, 1996) for a more detailed treatment of the book of Revelation.

4. Acts 7:56, Romans 8:34, Ephesians 1:20, Colossians 3:1, Hebrews 1:3, 8:1, 10:12, 1 Peter 3:22 and Revelation 4-5.

5. John 5:28-29, 6:39-40, 11:24, 1 Corinthians 15:50-54, 1 Thessalonians 4:15-17 and Hebrews 9:27.

Chapter 10—Like a Thief in the Night

1. Lewis, *The World's Last Night,* 105-106.

Chapter 11—Seize the Day

1. Lewis, *The World's Last Night,* 107.

Bibliography

BOOKS AND ARTICLES

Recommended

Bock, Darrell L., ed. *Three Views on the Millennium and Beyond.* Grand Rapids, Mich.: Zondervan Publishing House, 1999.

Boyer, Paul. *When Time Shall Be No More: Prophecy Belief in Modern American Culture.* Cambridge: Harvard University Press, 1992.

Clouse, Robert G., ed. *The Meaning of the Millennium: Four Views.* Downers Grove, Ill.: InterVarsity Press, 1977.

_____, Robert N. Hosack, and Richard V. Pierard, *The New Millennium Manual: A Once and Future Guide.* Grand Rapids, Mich.: Baker Books, 1999.

Ferguson, Gordon. *Mine Eyes Have Seen the Glory: The Victory of the Lamb in the Book of Revelation.* Woburn, Mass.: DPI, 1996.

_____. *Prepared to Answer.* Woburn, Mass.: DPI, 1995.

Garner, James Finn. *Apocalypse Wow! A Memoir for the End of Time.* New York: Simon & Schuster, 1997.

Grenz, Stanley J. *The Millennial Maze: Sorting Out Evangelical Options.* Downers Grove, Ill.: InterVarsity Press, 1992.

Heard, Alex. *Apocalypse Pretty Soon.* New York: W. W. Norton and Company, 1999.

Hendricksen, William. *More Than Conquerors.* Grand Rapids, Mich.: Baker, 1939.

Lewis, C. S. *The World's Last Night and Other Essays.* New York: Harcourt, Brace, and Company, 1988.

Examples of the Premillennial Mindset

Hagee, John. *Beginning of the End: The Assassination of Yitzhak Rabin and the Coming Antichrist.* Nashville: Nelson, 1996.

Jeffrey, Grant R. *Armageddon: Earth's Last Days,* revised and enlarged edition. Wheaton, Ill.: Tyndale House Publishers, Inc., 1997.

Jenkins, Jerry B. *Left Behind: A Novel of the Earth's Last Days.* Wheaton, Ill.: Tyndale House Publishers, Inc., 1995.

_____. *Millennium Meltdown.* Wheaton, Ill.: Tyndale House Publishers, Inc., 1998.

LaHaye, Tim. *Understanding the Last Days: The Keys to Unlocking Bible Prophecy.* Eugene, Oregon: Harvest House Publishers, 1998.

LaSor, William Sanford. *The Truth About Armageddon: What the Bible Says About the End Times.* Grand Rapids, Mich.: Baker, 1982.

Lindsey, Hal. *The Late Great Planet Earth.* Grand Rapids, Mich.: Zondervan, 1974.

_____. *Planet Earth: The Final Chapter.* Beverly Hills, Calif.: Western Front Ltd., 1998.

Y2K and Beyond

Farrar, Steve. *Spiritual Survival During the Y2K Crisis.* Nashville: Thomas Nelson Publishers, 1999.

Feldhahn, Shaunti Christine. *Y2K the Millennium Bug: A Balanced Christian Response.* Sisters, Oregon: Multnomah Publishers, 1998.

_____. *Y2K the Millennium Bug: Resource Guide.* Sisters, Oregon: Multnomah Publishers, 1999.

Hyatt, Michael S. *The Millennium Bug: How to Survive the Coming Chaos.* Washington, D.C.: Regnery Publishing, Inc., 1998.

Kellner, Mark A. "Y2K: A Secular Apocalypse?" *Christianity Today*, vol. 32, no. 1 (January 11, 1999) 60.

Lacey, Robert and Danny Danziger. *The Year 1000: What Life Was Like at the Turn of the First Millennium*. Boston: Little, Brown and Company, 1999.

Nussbaum, Debra. "Praying for a Year 2000 Solution," *The New York Times*, vol. CXLVIII, no. 51, 430 (February 11, 1999).

VIDEOS SHOWING THE PREMILLENNIAL MINDSET

Millennium 2000. Produced by Anthony J. Hilder. Indianapolis: Virtue International Publishing, 1996.

The Millennium Meltdown. Produced by Grant R. Jeffrey. Toronto, Canada: Frontier Research Publications, 1999.

INTERNET SITES THAT PROMOTED THE Y2K HYSTERIA

www.2000is.com
www.buy2000.co.uk
www.armageddonbooks.com
www.Cbn.org/y2k/index.asp
www.ccat.sas.upenn.edu/jod/avatars
www.channel1.com.mpr
www.dcf.org
www.garynorth.com
www.Itpolicy.gsa.gov/mks/yr2000/y2khome.htm
www.josephproject2000.org
www.juneau.com
www.kellner2000.com
www.mille.org
www.millenniumsociety.org

www.nccbuscc.org/jubilee/vatican/prayer.htm
www.rufftimes.com
www.survey2k.com
www.y2kprepare.com
www.y2ktimebomb.com
www.year2000.com

Who Are We?

Discipleship Publications International (DPI) began publishing in 1993. We are a nonprofit Christian publisher affiliated with the International Churches of Christ, committed to publishing and distributing materials that honor God, lift up Jesus Christ and show how his message practically applies to all areas of life. We have a deep conviction that no one changes life like Jesus and that the implementation of his teaching will revolutionize any life, any marriage, any family and any singles household.

Since our beginning we have published nearly 100 titles; plus we have produced a number of important, spiritual audio products. More than one million volumes have been printed, and our works have been translated into more than a dozen languages—international is not just a part of our name! Our books are shipped regularly to every inhabited continent.

To see a more detailed description of our works, find us on the World Wide Web at www.dpibooks.org. You can order books by calling 1-888-DPI-BOOK twenty-four hours a day. From outside the US, call 781-937-3883, ext. 231 during Boston-area business hours.

We appreciate the hundreds of comments we have received from readers. We would love to hear from you. Here are other ways to get in touch:

Mail: DPI, One Merrill St., Woburn, MA 01801
E-mail: dpibooks@icoc.org

Find Us on the World Wide Web

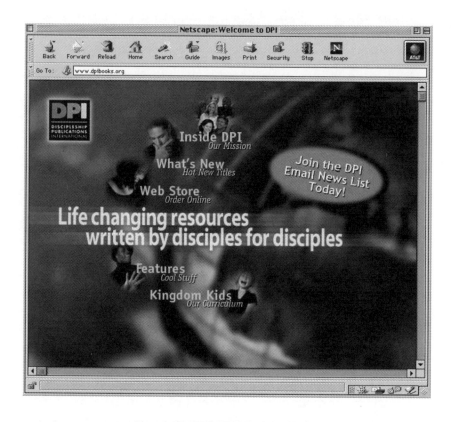

www.dpibooks.org
1-888-DPI-BOOK
outside US: 781-937-3883 x231